METROPOLITAN OPERA GUILD
COMPOSER SERIES

PUCCINI

the Man and his Music

WILLIAM WEAVER

Picture Editor: Gerald Fitzgerald

E. P. DUTTON
in association with
METROPOLITAN OPERA GUILD
New York

The illustrations in this book were made possible through the help of many generous people. The picture editor expresses deep appreciation to Rita Puccini, Simonetta Puccini, Biki, Albina del Panta, Wally Toscanini, Giampiero Tintori, Lorenzo Siliotto, Ferdinando G. Rizzi, Arnaldo Marchetti, Vittorio Giuliani, Adone Spadaccini, Angelo Ceresa, Eugenio Clausetti, Giuseppe Milani, William Weaver, Dorle Soria, George R. Marek, John W. Freeman, Mrs. John DeWitt Peltz, Mary Jane Matz and Nino Costa.

Library of Congress Cataloging in Publication Data | *Weaver, William, 1923–* | *Puccini.* | *(The Metropolitan Opera Guild composer series)* | *Bibliography: p.ix*| *1. Puccini, Giacomo, 1858–1924.* | *2. Composers—Italy—Biography.* | *I. Series: Metropolitan Opera Guild. The Metropolitan Opera Guild composer series.* | *ML410.P89W3   782.1'092'4 [B] 77-6324* | *ISBN: 0-525-18610-7* | *Published simultaneously in Canada by Clarke, Irwin & Company Limited, Toronto and Vancouver* | *Picture Editor and Captions by Gerald Fitzgerald* | *Project Coordinator, Leslie Carola* | *Production director David Zable* | *Text set by Pyramid Composition Company, Inc.* | *Display type set by Space Composers Group, Ltd.* | *Printed and bound by Dai Nippon Co., Ltd.* | *Designed by The Etheredges* | *10 9 8 7 6 5 4 3 2 1* | *First Edition*

Printed in Japan

CONTENTS

FOREWORD

THE Metropolitan Opera Guild Composer Series is an introduction to the lives of major composers whose works form the backbone of the opera repertory. Though designed for the general public, these brief, authoritative, illustrated books are a valuable addition to the library of every music-lover.

The authors are well-known authorities whose names are familiar to a nationwide public through association with the Saturday afternoon intermission broadcasts from the Metropolitan Opera.

Photographs and documentation have been selected by Gerald Fitzgerald, associate editor of *Opera News,* the magazine of the Metropolitan Opera Guild, and editor of the annual Guild calendars from which many of the illustrations are drawn. The stories of the operas were compiled by Stephen Wadsworth of *Opera News*.

The series was conceived by Dario Soria, managing director of the Metropolitan Opera Guild, and planned in conjunction with Leslie Carola of the Guild and the editors of E. P. Dutton.

THE PUBLISHERS

ACKNOWLEDGMENTS

IN retelling the story of Giacomo Puccini's life, I have naturally made use of previous versions of the story, especially those listed below.

MOSCO CARNER, *Puccini, A Critical Biography*. Duckworth, London, 1958.

EUGENIO GARA, *Carteggi Pucciniani*. Ricordi, Milan, 1958.

STANLEY JACKSON, *Monsieur Butterfly*. Stein & Day, New York, 1974.

GIORGIO MAGRI, *Puccini e le sue Rime*. Borletti, Milan, 1974.

ARNALDO MARCHETTI, *Puccini com'Era*. Curci, Milan, 1973.

GEORGE MAREK, *Puccini*. Simon and Schuster, New York, 1951.

LEONARDO PINZAUTI, *Puccini: una Vita*. Vallecchi, Florence, 1974.

VINCENT SELIGMAN, *Puccini among Friends*. Macmillan, New York, 1938.

I would also like to thank Dorle and Dario Soria for reading these pages in manuscript, and Geraldine Souvaine for encouraging my interest in Puccini by presenting me in many programs on Texaco's Saturday Matinee Metropolitan Opera Broadcasts.   WILLIAM WEAVER

Monte San Savino, October 1976

PICTURE CREDITS

PUCCINI

I

EARLY YEARS

GIACOMO Puccini had to be a composer. His father, grandfather, his ancestors for five generations had all been professional musicians and writers of music. Originally the family came from the Tuscan village of Celle, perched on a steep hill above the Val di Roggio; the Puccinis never lost contact with that lovely spot. Even after the first member of the family moved down to the plain, to the city of Lucca, at the beginning of the eighteenth century, there were still Puccinis who owned property in Celle, and there are still today.

When Giacomo was born, on December 22, 1858, his father, Michele, aged forty-five, had already sired five daughters. He was much respected as the city organist and choirmaster and as the composer of operas, symphonic works, besides the obligatory religious pieces. In 1864

Puccini's musical roots were deeply bedded in the hills of Tuscany. During the sixteenth century his ancestors settled in Celle, a hamlet situated over a verdant valley. The composer never lived there but felt strong familial ties with the place, revisiting it just before his death

Michele Puccini died; three months later a posthumous son was born and named Michele, after him.

Giacomo Puccini's mother, Albina Magi, was herself a musician and the sister of a musician, Fortunato, who became Giacomo's teacher. The uncle's instruction was apparently severe, and Magi had little faith in his nephew's gifts. Giacomo, oldest boy in a family largely composed of women, was unruly, refractory about studying. His mother decided what he needed was a new teacher. She sent him to Carlo Angeloni, a former pupil of her husband; under Angeloni's care, Giacomo's interest in his destined profession quickened.

Though Albina was not poor (despite her slim pension, the family always kept a servant), money was scarce, and Giacomo soon found his way to earning some. After being a choirboy in two of Lucca's churches he began playing the organ, at the age of fourteen, not only in Lucca but in some of the towns in the province, including Celle. According to legend, he also played the piano in a more unholy place. Perhaps it was there that he picked up the bad habit of smoking, which was to remain with him all his life and contribute probably to his fatal illness. Another legend has it that to pay for his cigarettes he sold some of the pipes of the San Paolino organ and, to disguise his theft, had to improvise very odd music during church services.

By the age of sixteen Giacomo was already composing, largely religious music. His teacher Angeloni had introduced him to opera—to Verdi, that is—through the study of published piano scores, and on March 11, 1876, Puccini heard his first opera in a theater. This was *Aida* in Pisa. Puccini and two music-loving friends, being chronically short of money, walked all the way to Pisa and back. The experience of *Aida* was crucial; it was probably on that evening that Puccini realized where his destiny lay. "I was born to write for the theater," he wrote later in his life. Lucca had lost an organist.

If opera was to be his career, Giacomo obviously had to go to the Italian operatic capital: Milan. After completing his studies at Lucca's Pacini Conservatory and writing a charming *Messa di Gloria* as his leaving-exercise, Giacomo was thinking of the Conservatory of Milan, the city where there was also La Scala and where, in 1880, Giuseppe Verdi was still alive, spending his winters at the Grand Hotel Milan. There was again the matter of money. But the resourceful Albina used influential friends to have Giacomo granted a royal scholarship, and she persuaded a bachelor uncle to supplement it. Giacomo's tuition for a three-year period was assured.

In Milan, Giacomo lived the bohemian life of a poor student. But he also moved in the most important musical and literary circles. In his first letter home (written sometime in November 1880), before he knew the outcome of his admission examination, he tells his mother he has been to see Alfredo Catalani, a fellow Lucchese, already an established composer. Catalani was a friend of Arrigo Boito, musician and future librettist of *Otello* and *Falstaff*. Another surviving letter of the period, dated December 18, 1880, finds Giacomo already studying at the Conservatory. "Yesterday I had my second lesson with Bazzini," he wrote, and continued, "I have arranged the following schedule for myself: I get up at 8:30 in the morning, and when I have a lesson I go there; otherwise I practice the piano a bit. I don't have to study much, but a little is necessary. . . . At 10:30 I have a light meal, then I go out. At one I go home and study for Bazzini a couple of hours; then between three and five, piano again and some reading of classical music. . . . At present I am playing through *Mefistofele* of Boito. . . . At five I go to my frugal (but very frugal!) supper and eat a minestrone alla milanese, which to be honest is very good. I eat three bowlfuls, then some other thing; a piece of cheese with *bei* and half a liter of wine. Afterward I light a cigar and go into the Galleria for a stroll up and down. . . . I stay there till nine, then come home dead

San Paolino in the prosperous city of Lucca, where five generations of Puccinis were composers. First of the dynasty was Giacomo I, born in 1712 (above). His great-great-grandson, the famous Giacomo, in his youth sold some of the church's organ pipes to purchase cigarettes. Among his early patrons was his great-uncle, Nicolao Cerù, a doctor who wrote a gossip column for a local paper (right)

tired. At home I do a bit of counterpoint. I don't play, because at night playing isn't allowed. Afterward I slip into bed and read seven or eight pages of a novel. That's my life."

Antonio Bazzini, one of Puccini's Milan teachers, had been a well-known concert violinist and had composed a fair body of music, including an opera based, curiously enough, on the Gozzi *Turanda* fable that was to crop up in Puccini's life many decades later. He was also, by all accounts,

an excellent teacher, and in 1882 he became head of the Conservatory. Puccini's other teacher was Amilcare Ponchielli, whose *La Gioconda,* staged at La Scala in 1876, had brought him fame and financial ease after a life of hardships. Ponchielli was an absent minded, generous man, who became Puccini's friend and mentor. He helped introduce the aspiring young composer into Milan's cultural life.

Legends also surround Puccini's early days in Milan. The most famous

At sixteen, Puccini studied at the Istituto Musicale Pacini. All personal mementos are now gone from the house in Lucca where he was born, but at the family home in Celle are the wreath he brought his dying mother after the premiere of Le Villi *and a bust of his father (top left). One can also see the kitchen (left), the great bed in which both he and his father first saw light, and his crib (above)*

concerns the brief period when he shared a room with a fellow-student, Pietro Mascagni, later to become famous with his *Cavalleria Rusticana*. Cooking meals in their room was strictly forbidden, so while one musician shuffled plates and pans, the other would improvise loudly at the piano to drown out the noise. It is easy to imagine how this carefree near-poverty was transfused into the pranks of the artists in *La Bohème*.

At the piano, Puccini composed as well. Works required by the Conservatory: fugues, an operatic scena "Mentì all'avviso" (text by Felice Romani), the first movement of a string quartet and—as his last school piece—an extended *Capriccio Sinfonico* for orchestra. This was conducted, at the Conservatory's final exercises in 1883, by Franco Faccio, leading conductor of the time (three years later he was Verdi's choice for the *Otello* premiere). And the composition was reviewed in glowing terms by the city's most important music critic, Filippo Filippi, who said, "In Puccini there is a definite and very rare musical talent, especially in orchestration. Unity of style, personality, character. . . . The ideas are clear, strong, highly effective."

Filippi's review appeared in *La Perseveranza* of July 15, 1883. Though he had his diploma in hand, Puccini did not rush home at once. He visited the Ponchiellis (the Signora Ponchielli was the famous soprano Teresina Brambilla) at their summer residence in Caprino Bergamasco. Nearby lived the poet and librettist Antonio Ghislanzoni (the young Puccini had already set a poem of his to music), whose house guest was another poet and dramatist, Ferdinando Fontana, eight years Puccini's senior and already established.

After the visit Puccini wrote his mother, from Milan, "I spoke with the poet Fontana . . . and we've almost settled for a libretto. In fact, he told me he liked my music, etc., etc. . . . There would be a nice little story that has been given to somebody else, but Fontana would prefer to

In 1880, at age twenty-two, Puccini enrolled at the conservatory in Milan. As today, the city's hub was the huge, glass-enclosed Galleria. When Puccini could afford it, he went there to drink coffee with friends and to stroll smoking a cigar. Nearby stood the Teatro alla Scala

give it to me instead. . . . In that way I could enter the Sonzogno competition." The Casa Sonzogno was an important Milanese publisher of books, magazines and music. That year it had announced a one-set opera competition (the next, in 1888, was to be won by *Cavalleria Rusticana*), and to the eager Giacomo this logically seemed a beckoning opportunity.

By August, Fontana and Puccini were both at work on *Le Willis* (the title was later Italianized to *Le Villi*). The libretto was finished in early September. In October—almost incidentally—Puccini's first published work appeared, a tender salon song, "Noi leggevamo insieme," as a supplement in Sonzogno's magazine *La Musica Popolare*. Puccini was probably too hard at work on his opera to pay much attention. He finished it in the nick of time, mailing it off from Lucca on December 31. Puccini's musical (and non-musical) handwriting was always difficult to decipher; the score of his first opera, written in haste, was an illegible mess. Early in 1884 the Sonzogno winners were announced. Puccini was not among them.

But the story of *Le Willis* did not end there. Shortly after the discouraging announcement, there was a musical evening in the home of Marco Sala, a well-to-do Milanese amateur of the arts. Puccini played excerpts from his opera for the guests, who included Arrigo Boito. At

Amilcare Ponchielli, composer of La Gioconda, *was once considered heir to Verdi's operatic throne. As professor of composition at the Royal Conservatory, he became mentor to Puccini. In 1883 the prodigy from Lucca sketched caricatures of his eccentric teacher on a student manuscript. His* Capriccio Sinfonico *earned him the school's bronze medal*

forty-two, Boito was an authoritative figure in Milan; his *Mefistofele,* after a rocky start, was now firmly in the repertory; he was a friend of the influential publisher Ricordi and, as everyone knew, was working closely with Verdi on *Otello.* As he had earlier helped Catalani, so he now took the young Puccini under his wing. With Fontana, Sala and others, Boito helped collect enough money to stage *Le Willis.* Ricordi printed the libretto free. Fontana and the composer made some opportune changes, and the opera was performed at the Teatro dal Verme on May 31, 1884, conducted by Arturo Panizza.

It was a triumph. "Applause for everything, absolutely everything," Filippi wrote in *La Perseveranza;* "the symphonic passage that ends the first part had to be played three times." And the *Corriere della Sera's* critic, Antonio Gramola, wrote, "We did not seem to have before us a young student but a Bizet, a Massenet." Marco Sala himself, in another paper, did not hesitate to call *Le Willis* a "masterpiece from beginning to end." And to set the seal on this success, Giulio Ricordi acquired the rights to the work and contracted with Puccini for another opera. Ricordi made the announcement in his magazine *La Gazzetta Musicale* of June 8, 1884: "The House of Ricordi herewith announces that they have acquired the rights to *Le Villi* for all countries . . . they have commissioned Maestro Puccini to compose a new opera to a libretto by Ferdinando Fontana. The new work will be given at La Scala." Puccini's success also attracted the attention of Verdi, on whom Ricordi no doubt pressed a score. The old man wrote to his friend Count Arrivabene, "I have heard the musician Puccini very well spoken of. He follows the modern tendency, which is only natural, but he remains attached to melody, which is neither modern nor ancient."

If the summer of 1884 brought Puccini the joy of artistic success, it also brought him a great sorrow. His mother, after a long illness, died on July 17. Summoned to her side, Puccini arrived in time to bid her good-bye and bring her the laurel wreath presented him at the final performance of *Le Willis*.

That same summer is crucial in his life for another reason. It was then that he and Elvira Bonturi decided to live together, though they could not marry (she was already married and the mother of two children, one of whom, Fosca, lived with Puccini and Elvira until her own marriage). Elvira's elopement with Giacomo obviously created many problems. His family, always somewhat strait-laced (one sister was a nun), was shocked and outraged. For the rest of his life Puccini was virtually an exile from Lucca. Though he later bought or rented houses in the area, he seldom visited the city itself. And, most pressingly, he found himself with a family to support.

Ricordi's contract included an advance against royalties, in the form of a monthly stipend. But it was barely enough to allow the young lovers a modest subsistence. For the first time in his life Puccini, cut off from home and family, had real financial problems. Among the results of the Lucca scandal was his uncle's demand that the loan be repaid. He also had musical problems. First, with Fontana's collaboration he revised *Le Willis* —now definitively rebaptized *Le Villi*—into two acts; on December 26, 1884, this new version was presented at the Teatro Regio in Turin, with fair success. A few weeks later Puccini made yet another, happy addition to the opera, the tenor aria "Torna ai felici dì," for the Scala presentation of the opera that same season, on January 24, 1885. The Scala audience, however, rejected the piece, which had a disastrous reception also in Naples a few months later.

Soon work was going forward on the next opera, a full-scale piece to be entitled *Edgar*. Its gestation was long, establishing a kind of tradition with Puccini, who—after *Le Villi*—was never to write an opera

rapidly or easily. Fontana's libretto has been severely criticized, but Puccini must accept equal responsibility for it, since he nagged the poet (as he was later to nag his other librettists) for modifications, additions, cuts. Actually, the libretto has a number of effective scenes and is surely no worse than many others. It was—as we can see now, with the wisdom of hindsight—a libretto hardly suited to Puccini's special gifts, though its Germanic story must have appealed to his Wagnerian tastes.

In any event, *Edgar* did not come to the stage until Easter Sunday, April 21, 1889. In those years Puccini and Elvira lived simply, for the

Elvira Bonturi Gemignani entered Puccini's life in 1884, soon after his mother's death. Wife of a classmate in Lucca, with two children, Elvira had beauty and a strong will. Defying scandal, she left her husband for Puccini, bearing him a son, Antonio, within two years. They were married in 1903

Ferdinando Fontana was the first
librettist of a Puccini opera,
Le Villi, which had its world premiere
on May 31, 1884, at Milan's Teatro
dal Verme (top right). Fontana is
seen here with the young composer.
Conductor for the first performance
was Arturo Panizza, who inspired a
poem: "Among conductors there's
Panizza / And Maestro Faccio, two of a
kind / One leads without the score /
Which pads the other's behind."
Shown here as well are costume
sketches for two of the characters
in Le Villi, Anna and Guglielmo Wulf

Tra quest chi, che l'è el Panizza
E'l maester Faccio, hin duu:
Vun el dirig senza la musega,
Quest la guarna sott al cuu.

most part in Milan. On December 23, 1886, their only child, Antonio, was born. Sustained by Ricordi, Puccini pinned all his hopes on *Edgar's* success. They were dashed by the Scala audience's tepid reception of the ambitious new piece.

Ricordi and La Scala had done their best. *Edgar's* conductor was Faccio; the contrasting female roles were sung by Aurelia Cataneo (the previous year she had been the first Italian Isolde, in Bologna) and Romilda Pantaleoni (Verdi's first Desdemona). The *Corriere's* review called the audience "cordial" and made it clear that *Edgar* was a near-failure. There were only three performances that season.

Shortly after the premiere Giulio Ricordi called Puccini and Fontana to his office. The discussion was long and heated, and the following morning the publisher sent the composer a letter. In the course of it he wrote, "Remember, Puccini, you are at a most difficult and critical time in your artistic life." Ricordi had some troubles of his own. The executives of his firm also called a meeting, to ask that the monthly payments to Puccini be curtailed. They suspected the young musician was a poor investment. Ricordi stood his ground, offering to repay his stockholders out of his own pocket if Puccini failed. As he wrote then to Puccini, "We will not fail. Stop worrying, get to work, look for a good subject and a good poet."

But first, that summer, Ricordi—who the previous year had acquired the Italian rights to Wagner's operas—sent Puccini to Bayreuth to hear *Die Meistersinger,* with a view to establishing cuts for Italian performances at La Scala the following season.

Edgar had some further performances in Italian cities with reasonable success, including one in Lucca, and it was given in Madrid in 1892 with a cast that included Tamagno (the creator of Verdi's Otello) and Luisa Tetrazzini.

Meanwhile, Puccini had chosen his new subject: the Abbé Prévost's

Romilda Pantaleoni, creator of Desdemona
in Verdi's Otello, portrayed Anna at
the first performance of Le Villi at
La Scala, Milan, on January 24, 1885.
(The soprano's costume closely matched
the original design, shown on the
preceding page.) By this time Puccini
had revised to two acts the one-act
version heard at the world premiere at
the Teatro dal Verme (playbill above).
In it Le Villi virtually duplicates
Adolphe Adam's popular ballet
Giselle: the spirit of a peasant girl
haunts the lover who has betrayed her

novel *Manon Lescaut*. The story of this opera's genesis is long and tortuous. The libretto and score were published without any librettist's name. The reason is that the final text is the result of many hands, including Puccini's and Ricordi's and probably Ruggiero Leoncavallo's. In any event, Puccini worked on the opera for about two years. It was finished in October 1892. This again was a crucial period in his life, marked by the death of his young brother Michele, a promising musician, who had gone

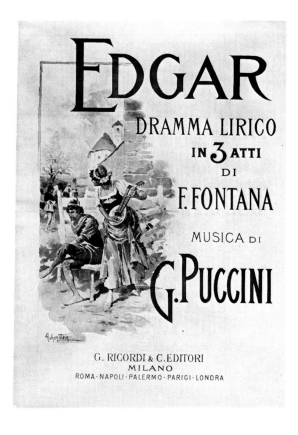

off to South America to seek his fortune, and by the lightning successes of his young contemporaries Mascagni (*Cavalleria*, 1890) and Leoncavallo (*Pagliacci*, 1892). Though Verdi himself was writing a new opera—*Falstaff* had its premiere only in 1893—he was obviously approaching the end of his career. The race for the succession was open, and it looked for a moment as if Puccini were going to be left behind. Everything depended on the outcome of this third opera of his.

An inane libretto by Fontana, about a fourteenth-century Flemish youth lured from true love by a gypsy temptress, spelled failure for Puccini's second opera, Edgar, which was given its world premiere at La Scala, Milan, on April 21. 1889. Still the critics praised the arias for the heroine, Fidelia, and Puccini maintained the faith of his publisher, Giulio Ricordi (above). Costume sketches shown at left are for Edgar and Fidelia

II

TRIUMPH

THE Teatro Regio in Turin during the last decade of the nineteenth century was one of Italy's most adventurous opera houses, thanks partly to the presence of the young Arturo Toscanini and partly, no doubt, to the nearness of Milan, which accentuated the Regio's rivalry with La Scala. After the near-failure of *Edgar,* it was logical for Ricordi and Puccini to think of a different theater for the launching of *Manon Lescaut.*

The opera's conductor was not Toscanini (whose association with Puccini would begin a few years later) but the gifted Alessandro Pome. In letters written before the premiere Puccini expressed his dissatisfaction with the cast, yet the title role was sung by Cesira Ferrani, whom he later chose to be his first Mimi in *La Bohème.* She and the other artists were,

Giorgio Lucchesi's oil catches a devil-may-care aspect of Puccini in days before fame. In fact he often suffered physical privation. While he composed Edgar, *he and Elvira subsisted on the small royalties earned by* Le Villi *and a monthly stipend of 300 lire paid by Ricordi*

in any event, warmly applauded by the capacity audience on opening night, February 1, 1893. The whole opera, for that matter, was enthusiastically received, the kind of total success Puccini was seldom to enjoy again in the rest of his otherwise successful career.

Alfredo Colombani, now the *Corriere della Sera* critic, wrote, "I have just come out of the Regio, very crowded, elegant, warm with enthusiasm, echoing the applause for *Manon Lescaut,* which won there a triumphal success. Although expectation was high, the opera surprised us thanks to its great artistic value, its powerful musical conception, its theatrical efficacy. . . . At first the public was alert but distrustful. Then that distrust was immediately disarmed by the value of the opera. The love, so human and yet so romantic, of Chevalier des Grieux for the sweet and naively depraved Manon lifted Puccini's talent to the sources of the most fresh and artistic inspiration. In fact, *Manon Lescaut* is an opera of passion and melody."

From Turin the opera moved to other Italian houses, and then abroad, laying the foundation of Puccini's international fame. In London, *Manon Lescaut* was heard at Covent Garden on May 14, 1894. One of its admirers was the critic G. B. Shaw, who wrote, "In Cavalleria and Pagliacci I can find nothing but Donizettian opera rationalized, condensed, filled in and thoroughly brought up to date; but in Manon Lescaut the domain of Italian opera is enlarged by an annexation of German territory. The first act, which is as gay and effective and romantic as the opening of any version of Manon need be, is also unmistakably symphonic in its treatment. . . . The act is really a single movement with episodes instead of being a succession of separate numbers, linked together. . . . Further, the experiments in harmony and syncopation, reminding one often of the intellectual curiosities which abound in Schumann's less popular pianoforte works, shew a strong technical interest which is, in Italian music, a most

Dressing up in costume was a favorite diversion of Puccini and his friends. Shown above, they give an improvised concert to celebrate the composition of La Bohème; *below, with Elvira joining the fun under the composer's watchful eye, they put on a scene from the play* La Figlia di Jorio

refreshing symptom of mental vigor . . . [the] poverty of the older masters made them so utterly dependent on the invention of tunes that they invented them better than the new men, who, with a good drama to work on, can turn out vigorous, imposing and even enthralling operas without a bar that is their own in the sense in which 'Casta Diva' is Bellini's own; but Puccini, at least, shews no signs of atrophy of the melodic faculty: he breaks out into catching melodies quite in the vein of Verdi: for example, 'Tra voi, belle,' in the first act of Manon, has all the charm of the tunes beloved by the old operatic guard. On that and other accounts, Puccini looks to me more like the heir of Verdi than any of his rivals."

The success of *Manon Lescaut* for Puccini meant, first of all, freedom from financial worries. Royalties began flowing in; he could pay back Ricordi; soon he would be a rich man. At this time his passion for acquiring houses began to make itself felt. As an act of filial piety he first bought back his birthplace, the family apartment in Via di Poggio, which had been sold after his mother's death. Then he started house-hunting along the Tuscan coast.

He had discovered the little locality of Torre del Lago in 1884. A bit inland from the Tyrrhenian Sea, the village—no more than a cluster of humble houses—is on the shore of marshy, beautiful Lake Massaciuccoli, which in addition to a romantic landscape offered an ideal location for shooting wild duck, pheasant, teal and the other victims of Puccini's passion for hunting.

At first Puccini rented part of an estate-keeper's house, then—as his situation improved and his requirements increased—he moved to a large nearby villa. At the same time, he kept a comfortable apartment in Milan.

And it was there that he began his next opera. Its birth was stormy. On March 21, 1893, just over a month after *Manon Lescaut*'s Turin

Marco Praga was among six librettists with whom Puccini fought to insure the quality of his third opera, which he based on the Abbé Prévost's novel Manon Lescaut. *Never again would he accept a weak text, as with* Edgar, *and he hired and fired versifiers, reducing some to tears*

premiere, Puccini wrote a letter to the editor of *Il Corriere della Sera,* which said, in part:

> The declaration in yesterday's *Secolo* by Maestro Leoncavallo must have made the public realize my complete good faith; because it is certain that if Maestro Leoncavallo, to whom for some time I have been bound by lively feelings of friendship, had told me before what he suddenly let me know the other evening, I would not then have thought of Mürger's *La Bohème.* Now—for reasons easily understood—it is too late for me to be as courteous as I would like toward a friend and a musician. For that matter, what does Maestro Leoncavallo care about this? Let him compose his opera and I will compose mine. . . . I want only to declare that for about two months, namely since the first performances of *Manon Lescaut* in Turin, I have been working seriously on my idea and have made no mystery about it with anyone.

The background of this curious letter is obscure. Apparently, on his return from Turin, Puccini ran into Leoncavallo in the Galleria and each

Giuseppe Cremonini and Cesira Ferrani portrayed the lovers in the world premiere of Manon Lescaut, *which was staged at the Teatro Regio in Turin on February 1, 1893. It was one of the few premieres at which Puccini was to enjoy an untarnished triumph. Three years later the composer chose Ferrani to sing the first Mimi in* La Bohème, *also in Turin. Tenor Cremonini went on to join the roster of the Metropolitan Opera, performing Mario Cavaradossi in the company's very first production of* Tosca, *in 1901*

composer told the other his new project, which proved to be the same: an opera drawn from Henri Murger's collection of sketches *Scenès de la vie de Bohème*, published in Paris almost half a century earlier. Leoncavallo immediately published a statement in *Il Secolo*, a newspaper owned by his publisher Sonzogno, and Puccini responded in *Il Corriere della Sera*. The battle was joined. Leoncavallo became Puccini's bitter enemy, even more so than another former friend, Mascagni.

In the letter quoted above, Puccini was being less than straightforward. He cannot have done much work, if any, on his *Bohème*, because his librettists had barely begun sketching the text. Both of these librettists had played, to a greater and lesser degree, a part in fashioning the tormented libretto of *Manon Lescaut*. Giuseppe Giacosa, playwright, essayist, poet, had had a look at it; Luigi Illica, also a playwright of distinction, had apparently made some revisions.

Now these two men together were to create the text for *La Bohème*,

forming with Ricordi and Puccini the successful if not always congenial team that would produce also *Madama Butterfly* and *Tosca:* the trio of Puccini's most successful works.

Giacosa, born in 1853, was older than Illica. A devoted husband and father, he was a sober member of the cultural establishment, a friend of Boito, of the novelist Antonio Fogazzaro, of the leading journalists and poets. Illica, born in 1857, was a more rebellious spirit: temperamental, quick to take offense but a gifted man of the theater. As a rule, Illica made the prose sketch of the work, cutting its dramatic form, while Giacosa then versified and polished. But the division of labor was not rigid. Relations between the two men were often strained, though Ricordi always managed to pour oil on the troubled waters of the collaboration.

In any case, it began well. Giacosa, after receiving Illica's first draft of the *Bohème* libretto, wrote him (on March 22, 1893), "I have read it and I admire you. You have been able to extract a dramatic action from

Manon Lescaut *was first heard at the Metropolitan Opera on January 18, 1907. Puccini himself was in the audience. Lina Cavalieri, a beauty once with the Folies Bergères of Paris, sang the heroine, with Antonio Scotti as her brother, Lescaut (above). Shown at left is the set for Act III*

a novel that to me always seemed exquisite but little-suited to dramatization. The first acts are stupendously composed. . . . I like the idea of collaborating with you, with your agile and wide-ranging spirit."

The collaboration was not only troubled. It was also long. Unlike Verdi, Puccini suffered from recurrent attacks of doubt; his self-confidence would abandon him, and he in turn would abandon the current work in progress. Some of these projects were cast aside for good; others were only temporarily dismissed, to be picked up later, then perhaps dropped once more. While Giacosa and Illica continued revising the libretto of *La Bohème,* Puccini at one point turned his attention away from the subject and began investigating an entirely different story: *La Lupa,* a successful novella by Giovanni Verga, the author of the original *Cavalleria Rusticana* story. Verga had dramatized both his stories with success, and obviously the rapid international triumph of Mascagni's opera drawn from the latter play had stimulated Puccini's interest in the former.

In the spring of 1894 Puccini traveled to Sicily, visiting Verga in Catania and discussing the idea with him. The composer also took some photographs of local sites and characters which he thought might come in handy (his passion for documentation had already begun). But on his voyage back north, Puccini discussed the Verga idea with a fellow-

passenger, Countess Blandine Gravina, daughter of Cosima Wagner. The lady persuaded him that the violent Sicilian story would bring him "nothing but misfortune," and the easily convinced composer wrote to Ricordi that he was assailed by "a thousand doubts."

At about this time Puccini began a kind of artistic flirtation with another leading light of Italian culture, the mercurial Gabriele D'Annunzio. But by the end of July 1894 Puccini had returned to *La Bohème* with renewed vigor and faith. Sometime in August, Illica wrote Ricordi, "It is Sunday, a quarter past twelve, and my eyes are moist. . . . Mimì has just died and the poor Bohemians are weeping, gathered in silence around her corpse. Tomorrow I'll finish the Latin Quarter [the present Act II of the opera]." And on January 12, 1895, Illica wrote Ricordi, "*Bohème* is —you might say—finished, and what is more important the Doge [a nickname given Puccini because of his autocratic manner] is satisfied with it." Puccini worked hard through the year, and by October the manuscript score was in the publisher's hands. That same month Ricordi wrote the composer, "*La Bohème* is now settled for Turin, then Rome."

Puccini was uneasy about the choice of Turin. The Regio's acoustics displeased him, and he thought it a mistake to tempt fate twice in the same place. Besides, Turin was uncomfortably close to Milan (where by now he had enemies in the musical world). But when he got to the Regio, he had at least one reason to rejoice: "Toscanini was very kind," he wrote Illica. The friendship between the composer and the twenty-eight-year-old conductor was immediate and profound; in later years it suffered occasional eclipses, but Toscanini remained devoted to the cause of Puccini's music throughout his long career.

La Bohème was first performed on February 1, 1896. It was a gala occasion, with members of the royal family in the audience as well as critics from all over Italy and a number of other composers, Mascagni

The tragic, final act of Manon Lescaut *takes place in a wasteland in Louisiana, where Des Grieux and Manon have fled to escape the authorities. Shown here is the heroine's death scene as staged at the Metropolitan in 1973, with Gilda Cruz-Romo as Manon and Carlos Montané as the despairing Des Grieux* among them. Though there were curtain calls at the end of each act, the evening was not happy for Puccini, who recalled it years later: "The audience had received the opera well. The critics the next day spoke ill of it. But even that night, between acts, in the corridors and backstage I heard whispering around me: 'Poor Puccini! This time he's on the wrong track! This is an opera that won't long survive.' I felt in me a sadness, a melancholy, a desire to cry. . . . I spent a bad night. And the next morning I received the spiteful greeting of the newspapers."

The worst of the newspapers was Turin's own *Gazzetta Piemontese*, whose critic Carlo Bersezio wrote, "Just as *La Bohème* leaves slight impression in the spirit of its listeners, so it will leave a scant trace in the history of our opera, and the author would be well advised to consider it a passing error."

Other critics were less severe, but none was openly, totally enthusiastic. Curiously, Puccini, so unsure of himself while writing his operas, gained confidence in adversity. And the public soon proved him right. In Turin there were twenty-four performances in rapid succession; *La Bohème* won ovations in Rome, Naples and especially Palermo.

If *Manon Lescaut* was Puccini's first really successful opera from a commercial point of view, *La Bohème* was his first complete artistic success. With this work, the "Puccini style" was completely fused; the tunes, the orchestration are already "Puccinian." Even more than its predecessor, *La Bohème* quickly became an international favorite. Shortly after Palermo, Buenos Aires heard it. Then London and Paris. Puccini, too, was becoming internationally famous. He took great pains over each important foreign premiere, often traveling great distances (eventually even to New York) to supervise details of production and rehearsal. Though he never learned to speak a foreign language well or to move easily in smart society, Puccini—thanks to his music and despite himself—became literally a man of the world.

During the 1950s and 1960s, the Metropolitan Opera's most frequent interpreter of Des Grieux in Manon Lescaut *was Richard Tucker. Also noted for his Rodolfo, Mario Cavaradossi, Pinkerton, Dick Johnson and Calaf, the American tenor always considered Des Grieux his favorite role*

III

TROUBLES AND
TOSCA

IN 1896, at the time of *La Bohème,*
Puccini was in his late thirties. He had put on weight, but he was still
handsome, popular with both men and women. At home, which was now
Torre del Lago, with some local friends—mostly penniless, jolly painters
—he had formed a Club La Bohème, whose clubhouse was a thatched
shack on the lake and whose aim was having a good time, hunting, eating,
joking. Perhaps even earlier Puccini had begun his extracurricular amours,
which were to arouse the terrible, justified jealousy of Elvira. Until his
last years his home life was almost always unhappy, sometimes dramati-
cally so. As if to compensate, he traveled. More than other composers,
he followed his operas as they made their first appearance in one city or
another. A few months after the *Bohème* premiere in Turin, Puccini was

*Leontyne Price is among the illustrious sopranos who have
starred in* Manon Lescaut *at the Metropolitan Opera. (A new
production of Puccini's work was also staged for her in 1974
by the San Francisco Opera.) Her Met predecessors include
Lucrezia Bori, Dorothy Kirsten, Licia Albanese, Renata Tebaldi*

in Palermo supervising the first production there. He also watched over the first production at La Scala, and in 1898 he went to Paris twice, to arrange and then to attend the French premiere of *La Bohème* at the Opéra Comique.

But as he wrote to a friend in Lucca, "I'm fed up with Paris. I long for the woods . . . I long for the free swaying of my belly in loose trousers, with absence of 'gilet'; I long for the sea wind . . . I hate pavements! . . . I hate steam, top hat, evening dress."

The French premiere of *Bohème* was a triumph, and Puccini took advantage of his stay in Paris (where the librettist Illica joined him) to carry out an important mission. For some time the composer and his librettists had been at work on a new opera, to be derived from the successful Sarah Bernhardt vehicle *La Tosca* by Victorien Sardou. Bernhardt had toured Italy in the play, and Puccini and Elvira had seen her in it in Florence in October 1895; but Puccini had been interested in the subject even before then.

Now, with *Bohème* happily on its way through the world, he was ready to start again. There was a problem: *Tosca* had been promised to another composer, Alberto Franchetti (a former pupil of Puccini's father). Ricordi—who by now was eager to foster Puccini's career, even at the expense of another Ricordi composer—persuaded Franchetti to cede the libretto rights to Puccini. .

But Sardou, from Paris, had to approve any modifications of his text (which first of all had to be drastically shortened); now an elderly, revered man of the theater, he was notoriously difficult. At their meeting, he asked Puccini to play some of the music of *Tosca,* not a note of which had yet been written. Puccini obliged by improvising a medley of tunes from his earlier operas, and Sardou was satisfied (he was more satisfied once the financial terms were settled, giving him a royalty of 15 percent).

In the summer of 1898, to work in greater seclusion, Puccini took a house in the remote region of Monsagrati. Elvira and Fosca hated it; even Puccini wrote to Ricordi, "Hot! hot! hot! I sleep during the day and work at night. . . . I am in an ugly, hateful spot, among forests and pines where the view is blocked, barred by mountains . . . blazing sun, without any wind. I work from ten until four in the morning. . . . I am really content to have taken refuge in this boring place where the human being is the exception. . . . I hope to stay here till October (I say I hope because I don't know if I'll hold out)."

Work proceeded through the autumn, with the usual moments of ill-humor among the librettists, pacified as usual by Ricordi. And there were the familiar demands from Puccini for changes, additions and subtractions. At one point, someone—either Giacosa or Ricordi himself—removed from the opera its most famous line, "E avanti a lui tremava tutta Roma." Puccini wisely had it reinstated.

In January 1899 he paid another visit to Paris and to Sardou, who was surprised to learn, among other things, that the Tiber did not flow between Castel Sant'Angelo and St. Peter's. "Oh, that's nothing," he said to Puccini, who reported back to Ricordi. By that autumn the opera was virtually finished, and Puccini was writing to his friend Alfredo Vandini to find him a Roman poet who could write some dialect verses to insert in the opera. The poet was found—Luigi Zanazzo—and the verses were written, becoming the haunting, offstage shepherd's song of the last act.

Then on October 10, 1899, when the opera was really complete, a bolt from the blue: Ricordi wrote to Puccini saying, "With all frankness and in good conscience I have the courage to say to you [that] the third act of *Tosca,* as it stands, seems to me a grave error both in conception and in writing . . . such a grave error that in my view it would erase the interesting impression of Act I! It would erase the very powerful

Giuseppe Giacosa and Luigi Illica, two of the librettists who helped write Manon Lescaut, *were hired for Puccini's next opera,* La Bohème, *based on Murger's novel. As they worked on the new text, a feud erupted between Puccini and another of the* Manon Lescaut *librettists, Ruggiero Leoncavallo, then at work composing his own version of* La Bohème, *which is seldom performed. Leoncavallo's fame was to rest on another work,* Pagliacci

Puccini's manuscripts were messy and filled with doodles, the Schaunard-Colline duel in La Bohème *sporting a self-portrait (right). Some critics found the opera trivial at its premiere, in Turin's Teatro Regio, February 1, 1896. Musetta that night was Camilla Pasini, and Arturoi Toscanini conducted (far right)*

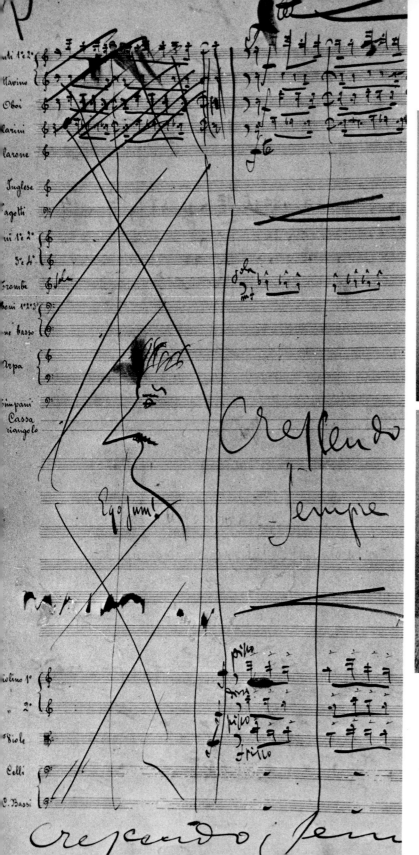

emotion that will certainly be aroused by Act II, a genuine masterpiece of efficacy and tragic expression!!"

Then Ricordi became specific: "Cavaradossi's scene, Tosca's entrance are beautiful and effective—just as the shooting and the end are effective and a fine invention. But good God . . . what is the real, luminous center of this act? The Tosca-Cavaradossi duet. What do I find? . . . a fragmentary duet, with little lines that diminish the characters; I find one of the most beautiful passages of lyric poetry, that of the hands, underlined only by a melody, also fragmentary and modest, and what's more a piece taken *talis et qualis* from *Edgar*!!! . . . In short, what should have been a kind of hymn . . . a hymn of love, reduced to a few bars! . . . . Where is that Puccini of the noble, warm, vigorous inspiration?" Throughout this remarkable letter, Ricordi protested his profound, paternal affection for Puccini, and the sincerity of the publisher's words is evident and moving.

Puccini, from Torre del Lago, answered the next day: "Your letter was an extraordinary surprise to me! I am still affected by it. Nevertheless, I am serene and convinced that if you play through that third act again your opinion will change! No, this is not pride on my part. It's the conviction of having portrayed as best I could the drama that was before me. . . . As for the fragmentary quality, that is deliberate: this cannot be a uniform and tranquil situation as in other love conversations."

Puccini also wrote affectionately, but he—often a vacillator, a waverer —stood his ground. The third act of *Tosca* remains as he wrote it.

For the premiere of *Tosca*—a Roman story—the Teatro Costanzi in Rome was chosen. The designer was Adolfo Hohenstein, who worked regularly at La Scala and had designed, a few years before, the sets of Verdi's *Falstaff*. Tito Ricordi—Giulio's son—was to supervise the staging, and the cast included the beautiful Rumanian soprano Hariclea Darclée in the

44

Despite initial reservations, La Bohème *became indispensable to the repertory. In recent years a production conceived by Franco Zeffirelli has assumed classic status at La Scala, Milan. Here are Acts I and III at La Scala, with Mirella Freni as the seamstress Mimi and Gianni Raimondi as the poet Rodolfo*

In 1900, when La Bohème *was first heard at the Metropolitan Opera, critic Henry Krehbiel judged it "foul in subject . . . futile in its music." Today only Verdi's* Aida *outranks Puccini's romance in popularity. At right are Katia Ricciarelli as Mimi and José Carreras as Rodolfo during the heroine's touching death scene. Below, a droll cariacature of* La Bohème's *composer*

Act II of the Metropolitan Opera's 1977 staging of La Bohème, *with Maralin Niska (Musetta), Ingvar Wixel (Marcello), Renata Scotto (Mimi), Luciano Pavarotti (Rodolfo), Paul Plishka (Colline), Allan Monk (Schaunard)*

title role, with Emilio de Marchi—a leading verismo tenor—as Mario, and the twenty-eight-year-old baritone Eugenio Giraldoni, all three excellent actors. The conductor was Leopoldo Mugnone, the fiery Neapolitan who had conducted the premiere of *Cavalleria Rusticana* a decade earlier in that same theater.

Italy at the turn of the century was an uneasy country. In the last decade of the 1800's there had been a peasant outbreak in Sicily, the rise of the Socialist Party (feared by many as a mob of bomb-throwing anar-

Renata Scotto sang Musetta (right) and Mimi at the Metropolitan Opera during the 1976-1977 season in a production designed by Pier Luigi Pizzi that was borrowed from the Lyric Opera of Chicago. Both companies featured the Italian tenor Luciano Pavarotti as Rodolfo, but in Chicago he was paired with the Mimi of Rumanian soprano Ileana Cotrubas (far right). The set shown here is the garret of Acts I and IV

chists) and the continuation of wearing, often humiliating fighting in East Africa. Prime Minister Pelloux had tried to suppress constitutional liberties, and grievances were many. The unrest was to culminate, only six months after *Tosca*'s premiere, with the assassination of King Umberto at Monza.

That uneasiness was felt in Rome on the night of January 14, even inside the Teatro Costanzi, where the queen—an ardent music-lover—was expected to be sitting in the royal box. The police had received a bomb

threat, and Mugnone had been instructed that in case of a disturbance he was to strike up the national anthem. Fortunately, Mugnone—hardly encouraged by this advice—kept the news from the nervous Puccini.

The audience, too, was nervous; it included not only Roman dignitaries but the major representatives of the new generation of Italian composers, the "young school": Mascagni, Cilea, Franchetti.

The first act went well, and the tenor's aria "Recondita armonia" had to be repeated, along with the entire finale, after which the composer was called out twice. In the second act, "Vissi d'arte" was repeated, and Puccini had one call. He was called out again after the "dawn" scene of the last act, and three times at the end. Less than a triumph. The critics, too, made severe observations about the music and, even more, about the libretto, which many considered unsuited to Puccini's temperament.

But the public liked it and filled the Costanzi for twenty more performances. From there *Tosca* moved to other Italian cities, and—in July of that same year—to London, where it was given at Covent Garden with Milka Ternina in the title role and Antonio Scotti for the first time as Scarpia, a part that was to become perhaps his most famous interpretation.

Puccini—more and more a world traveler—journeyed to London for the occasion and wrote this description to his Lucca friend Alfredo Caselli: "LONDON, six million inhabitants (and that's a lot!), immense, infernal, indescribable movement. Paris nothing in comparison. Language impossible, women very beautiful, shows splendid, and . . . all the pastimes you want. A city not very beautiful but fascinating."

Then, after similar succinct descriptions of Paris, Manchester, Brussels, and Milan, he concluded, "TORRE DEL LAGO, supreme bliss, paradise, Eden, empyrean, 'turris eburnea,' 'vas spirituale,' palace . . . inhabitants 120, houses twelve. . . ." By August he was back there, and in despair. He was, as he used to say during such periods, "out of work." He had

Many a singer has made his or her debut at the Metropolitan Opera in La Bohème, *an almost certain way to win the heart of the public. Among the best-loved are Jussi Bjoerling, who introduced his Rodolfo to New York in 1938, and Mirella Freni, who brought her Mimi here during the 1965-66 season*

asked Zola to give him *L'Abbé Mouret* for an opera and received a negative answer. Illica wanted him to set a *Marie Antoinette,* which Puccini had already toyed with, but as he wrote Ricordi the French Revolution background was "trite and exploited." "I don't know where to turn," he continued. "The best years of my life (the last of youth) are passing. It's a shame."

Puccini was in his early forties, but the reference to advancing age was not casual. He felt older than his years, and did indeed age prematurely. So far, on the whole, his life had been happy and successful; now he was to know failure and tragedy.

IV

FIASCO

For the rest of his life Puccini spent more of his time searching for librettos than writing music. The composition of each of his operas—a long and painful process in itself—was regularly preceded by frantic examination of books, stories, sketches, sometimes with momentary bursts of enthusiasm, quickly spent; on other occasions with longer interest, which dwindled only gradually. After *Tosca* Puccini thought not only of Zola and Marie Antoinette; there were extended flirtations with Daudet's *Tartarin de Tarascon* and Benjamin Constant's *Adolphe,* and more than a flicker of interest in a libretto based on the life of St. Margaret of Cortona.

But during that summer of 1900, when Puccini was in London for *Tosca,* he went to the Duke of York's Theater (though he knew not a

Magda Olivero made a fiery debut at the Metropolitan Opera as Tosca on April 3, 1975, dispatching Scarpia with a single knife thrust. For two generations she had been Italy's preferred interpreter of Puccini heroines—Manon, Mimi, Tosca, Cio-Cio-San, Minnie, Giorgetta, Suor Angelica, Lauretta, Liù

word of English) to see Evelyn Millard in *Madame Butterfly,* a play by David Belasco and John Luther Long based on a novella of Long's. According to Belasco's unreliable memoirs, Puccini immediately asked permission to turn the story into an opera. Actually, the composer's interest in the subject developed more slowly. It was only later, after his return to Italy, that he instructed Ricordi to inquire about the rights to "that American subject." And it was only in March 1901 that he finally sent Illica a translation of the original story. He wrote the librettist then, saying, "Read it and tell me what you think. I'm completely taken with it."

Illica's reaction was favorable, but Ricordi was cold to the notion. This coldness only fed Puccini's flame. He urged Illica to convey his interest to Ricordi, so the librettist duly wrote the publisher: "For three days I have been in Nagasaki. I've made the acquaintance of the famous marriage broker, who wears, however, a European suit, which seems to be a good idea. I've also introduced myself to the American consul, a bluff, jovial man, good, at heart philosophical and, after living in various countries, scornful of all fads and customs, appreciating now only good people, whether they be English or Boers, Americans or Japanese. . . ."

The choice was made. It was to be *Butterfly,* and Illica had to set to work immediately. As Puccini wrote him on April 7, the final agreement had been made with Belasco. In May a copy of the story was sent also to Giacosa, who once again was to collaborate on the text. Giacosa was in poor health and worked slowly, arousing the composer's impatience. In return, as before, Giacosa irritably threatened to quit the whole project.

Illica's enthusiasm was tempered by doubts, which he expressed to Ricordi (the four-way correspondence of librettists, composer and publisher makes fascinating, if complex, reading): "Here is Puccini's error: it is believing that the drama of *Butterfly* consists of the scenic details confected by Belasco. To be sure, they made the first, immediate impression on him. . . . But look at the matter of the tenor; Pinkerton is unlikable! Once introduced . . . he isn't seen again. [His reappearance in the last scene was invented by the opera's librettists] . . . But finally Illica said, "Believe me, *Butterfly* is the strongest thing Puccini has ever had, strong and new, but not easy! . . . also the most suited to Puccini, to his elegance."

On June 2 Puccini wrote to Illica, "Sig. Giulio, after the reading, was completely won over. He told me he couldn't sleep afterward." Then the letter ends with a sentence that was to prove ominous: "I won't have the automobile until about the 20th of June. . . ."

Puccini loved machines. One of his first purchases, when he became financially independent, was a very fancy bicycle. Then, after *Bohème,* he bought the *Mimì I,* the first of a series of motorboats he used on Lake Massaciuccoli and along the Tuscan coast. Naturally, the newfangled automobile appealed to him. His first purchase was a Buire, but he soon had more than one car, and he enjoyed touring with Elvira, Fosca, his son Tonio and their chauffeur, Guido.

Butterfly was proceeding promisingly though slowly. Puccini collected some Japanese music, some Japanese phonograph records (now preserved in the Puccini Museum in the family house at Celle), and even consulted a popular Japanese actress, Sada Yacco. The composer had trouble with his librettists when he decided to suppress a second act that was to have been set in the U.S. Consulate, but by February 1903 all seemed well. And on the 21st of that month he wrote Illica from Milan, "I'm leaving now for Torre for five or six days with Elvira, by car. God be with us! I'll write you the outcome. . . ."

The drive to Torre went off safely, but a few days later Puccini had to drive to Lucca to see a doctor about a persistent throat ailment. After having dinner with friends, the Casellis, the party set off for home—

Puccini, Elvira, Tonio and the chauffeur. It was a foggy night, and the roads were icy. When they had gone about four miles from Lucca, the car skidded off the road and crashed down fifteen feet into a field. Elvira and Tonio suffered only shock. The driver, thrown from the car, fractured a thigh. But Puccini was trapped under the overturned car itself, half-poisoned by the fumes of the leaking fuel tank. It took the others some time to find him. Luckily a doctor lived nearby. Having heard the racket of the car, he had looked out his window, seen the accident and hurried to the spot. Puccini was taken first to his house, where a fractured shin was diagnosed and treated. From there he was moved on a stretcher to the house of another friend, Marchese Ginori Lisci, on the inland side of Lake Massaciuccoli. The marchese and his family helped the injured composer onto a barge and ferried him across the lake to his house.

Melodrama was rampant at the world premiere of Tosca, *which took place at the Teatro Costanzi in Rome on January 14, 1900. A bomb threat alarmed the conductor, who fled the podium when a hostile claque began shouting invective. But he returned, order was restored, and* Tosca *earned genuine esteem. Eugenio Giraldoni (left), who sang the role of Baron Scarpia, provided the onstage menace. The famous Ricordi poster for* Tosca *shown here, the work of Austrian scenic designer Adolf Hohenstein, reflects the grandeur of the Belle Epoque*

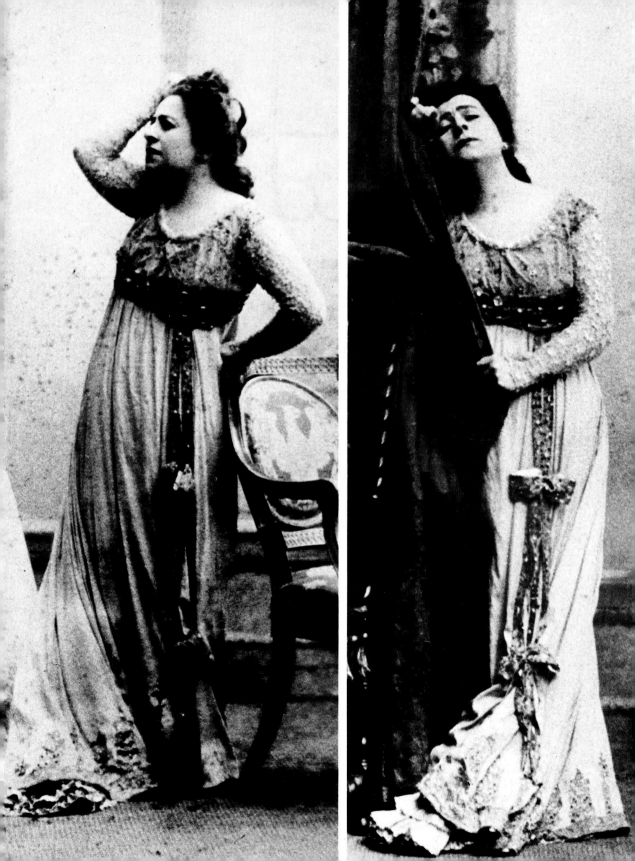

The celebrated Rumanian
diva Hariclea Darclée,
who created the title
roles in Catalani's La Wally
and Mascagni's Iris, was
the first soprano to suffer
the torments of the
operatic Tosca. Her role
in the drama was fixed by
the awesome precedent of
Sarah Bernhardt, the flamboyant
actress who had inspired
Victorien Sardou to write
his play La Tosca, from which
Puccini's libretto is drawn.
The composer met the playwright
in Paris to discuss the project
but instead of insight he was
treated to long-winded,
boring anecdotes that proved
of little value to his work.
Still, compressing the play's
original five-act length to
the opera's three acts, the composer
lost not an iota of the
power and passion of Sardou's
now forgotten opus—forgotten
except as it survives through
the genius of Puccini

"*Carissimo* Illica," he wrote on March 1, "this is from my bed, where I will remain, I am told, two months."

Puccini's healing was instead to be long and painful. For the rest of his life the composer walked with a slight limp. Moreover, during the course of his examinations and treatment it was discovered that he had diabetes.

But by September 1903 he was back at work. "I've finished the 'berceuse,'" he wrote Illica on the 3rd, "and I'm at the Sharpless-Pinkerton-Suzuki trio. I've already jotted down part of the last scene where Butterfly speaks to the child before dying. Still I have to orchestrate all this eternal second act. Will it be too long? I haven't yet measured it, but I fear it lasts well over an hour. . . ."

Puccini, now more or less well, was not only working. He was carrying on, as he often did, an extramural affair, which Elvira knew about. Recently published letters of Elvira (in Marchetti's *Puccini com'era*) refer to "that maleficent person," and in one she says, "He wanted to drive me out (and he had Ricordi tell me so), promising that he would join me yesterday or today at the latest; today instead he writes that he doesn't know when he'll be back! . . . I have done everything I could to end this story, I humiliated myself, I pleaded, but since it has served nothing, I have decided on a separation."

Instead, on January 3, 1904, Puccini and Elvira were finally married legally, since her first husband, Narciso Gemignani, had died the previous February.

A month later Puccini was in Milan, where *Butterfly* was in rehearsal at La Scala. This was the composer's first premiere at the theater since the ill-starred *Edgar,* and it was obviously a significant choice. Again, things had been carefully organized by Ricordi. The cast was first-rate: the lovely Rosina Storchio as Butterfly; Giovanni Zenatello, Pinkerton; and Giuseppe

The Metropolitan Opera introduced Tosca *on February 4, 1901, with Antonio Scotti (below) in the first of his 156 Scarpias there. After 1921 his most frequent Tosca was Maria Jeritza, who scrapped with one Mario, Beniamino Gigli (left). During a bow she told the public, "Mr. Gigli is not nice with me!"*

De Luca, Sharpless. The sets were by the illustrious French artist Jusseaume. The conductor was Cleofonte Campanini. A few hours before curtain time Puccini sent a note to his soprano: "*Cara* Rosina, any good wishes of mine are futile! Your great art is so true, delicate, impressive that the public will surely be mastered by it! And I, thanks to you, hope to hasten to victory!"

Puccini's confidence in victory was real. From Lucca he had invited his sisters to attend, and his son Tonio—now eighteen—was (excep-

In 1964, Franco Zeffirelli directed a memorable new production of Tosca *at London's Royal Opera, Covent Garden, that featured a dynamic trio of stars—Tito Gobbi as Baron Scarpia, Maria Callas as Floria Tosca and Renato Cioni as Mario Cavaradossi. Here they are in the tension-filled second act*

tionally) allowed to stand with him backstage.

Instead of victory, the family witnessed a fiasco. One journalist described the public's reaction: "Groans, explosions, lowing, laughter, shouting, snickering, the usual solitary cries of *bis* deliberately meant to enrage the spectators further: this, in synthesis, is the welcome of the Scala's audience to the new work of Maestro Giacomo Puccini. After this pandemonium the public left the theater happy as can be, and never were such merry faces seen, so joyously content in their collective triumph."

One of the members of the family present was Puccini's beloved sister Ramelde, who wrote that same night to her husband, Raffaello Franceschini: "You can imagine in what a state I am writing you. We [Ramelde had gone to Milan with her little daughter Alba] are more dead than alive. I don't know what I'm writing. I'm in bed. It's 4 A.M. We went to bed at 2, and I can't close my eyes. And when I think how confident we all were! Giacomo didn't even talk about the opera. We went there with very little apprehension, and luckily we were in a box, otherwise we would have made a spectacle of ourselves, we were so distraught. The audience was hostile from the beginning. We realized that at once. . . . Disgusting public, base, cowardly. Not even a sign of respect. Giacomo, two hours ago, after the theater, had regained his strength. . . . Giacomo is convinced he did a good job and he hopes the opera will be salvaged. . . . Don't show or discuss this letter. . . . If anybody asks, say that Giacomo calmly says the public was severe, but he is convinced he did a good job, indeed that this is his best opera."

La Scala's audience had been ignorantly severe before (with Bellini's *Norma*) and since, but in all fairness it must be said that the *Butterfly* they mocked is not the *Butterfly* popular all over the world today. Even in his anguish Puccini realized changes had to be made. In the first place, the work was too long; the second act, about whose length the composer had in fact expressed concern, lasted an hour and a half, its two scenes played without intermission.

The morning after the premiere, in Puccini's apartment in Via Verdi, the street that flanks La Scala, there was a meeting: Puccini, the Ricordis father and son, Illica, Giacosa and Rosina Storchio. They decided to withdraw the opera at once. Publisher and author would return their share of the first night's proceeds (the substantial sum of 20,500 lire) to La Scala. And Puccini would revise the opera.

The Metropolitan Opera's first Tosca, in 1901, was a commanding personality from Yugoslavia, Milka Ternina (left), a soprano renowned for Wagner roles. Over half a century later, in 1955, her no less commanding protégée, Zinka Milanov (right), added Tosca to her many Met roles, which included Norma, Aida and La Gioconda

Puccini's first changes were mostly cuts, but he also made some significant additions, including Butterfly's dramatic outburst "Trionfa il mio amor" on the sighting of Pinkerton's ship. For that matter, the part of Butterfly suffered least in the pruning; it was instead some of the Belasco-like condiments that were removed.

On May 28 the new version of *Butterfly* was given at the Teatro Grande in Brescia, a small city not far from Milan. The audience was as much Milanese as Brescian, but this time it reversed its opinion (justifying also Puccini's contention that the Milanese fiasco was organized by his enemies, of whom—as Italy's most successful living composer—he now had many). In any event, the opera's success now matched or even surpassed that of its predecessors.

Like them, it soon went abroad and Puccini also seemed seized by a fierce wanderlust. With Elvira he journeyed (for a sizable fee) all the way to South America to attend a season of his operas, including the almost forgotten *Edgar,* revived for the occasion. He went to Paris, and—without Elvira—to London.

Here he met the beautiful, fascinating Sybil Seligman, wife of a wealthy banker. A lion-hunter and a gifted amateur musician, Sybil had little difficulty in winning the expansive Puccini. Biographers disagree as to the exact nature of their friendship. It seems likely that it began as a love affair but soon relaxed and mellowed into a profound friendship. Sybil was even able to make friends with the increasingly jealous Elvira. And Puccini relied on this cultivated, witty Englishwoman for all sorts of advice, both marital and operatic. His letters to her, many of them including jokes in his idea of English, are among the most engaging and revelatory he wrote. One of his ways of signing them was "Noti Boi" (Naughty Boy).

Composition proved grueling for Puccini and he looked for
excuses to escape the drudgery. Once, in his garden at
Torre del Lago, he and a colleague acted out his dilemma,
putting their heads in a laundry press to squeeze out inspiration.
Another diversion—automobiles, his first a 1900 Buire

V

TRAGEDY AND
THE GIRL

THE years that followed *Madame Butterfly* were the most unhappy of Puccini's life. On the surface he had everything a man could want: wealth, fame, success both in his work and in his philandering. He had lost some weight and was more handsome than ever, as the many photographs and portraits of him bear witness. But his success was tainted by the envy of his colleagues or his suspicion of them, and by a growing opposition to his music among younger critics (to culminate in a famous attack, *Giacomo Puccini e l'opera internazionale* by Fausto Torrefranca, published in 1912). His domestic life was daily becoming more infernal, thanks to his own irrepressible womanizing and Elvira's violent jealousy, which led Puccini's bohemian friends to call her the "policeman."

A serene lakefront villa at Torre del Lago in Tuscany was built by Puccini in 1900, and here he lived until 1922. Now owned by the composer's daughter-in-law, Rita Puccini, it has become a public museum, tended with a blend of love and scholarship by her and Puccini's granddaughter, Simonetta

And, of course, he was out of work. Again the anguished search for a libretto began. He told some American journalists that he was thinking of a *King Lear* or a *Benvenuto Cellini*. He asked Giacosa to find him a comic subject. He even played with the notion of a *William Tell*. At Ricordi's urging he had several meetings with Gabriele D'Annunzio, then at the height of his fame. The word-spinning poet presented him with a *Parisina* (later set, with disastrous results, by Mascagni) and, when Puccini turned that down, *La Rosa di Cipro,* which proved equally unusable. Sybil got him briefly interested in an Oscar Wilde play, *A Florentine Tragedy,* and Strauss' success with Wilde's *Salomé* led Puccini to give the project serious attention. Even more serious was a long attraction to a novel by Pierre Louÿs, *La Femme et le Pantin,* a Spanish story with a fatal heroine who has some qualities in common with Mérimée's *Carmen.* Puccini actually got Ricordi to acquire the rights. In Paris the composer had long conferences with Louÿs and Maurice Vaucaire, who had made a highly successful French dramatization of the story. Illica was commissioned to do the libretto (Giacosa was ailing and died in 1906, to Ricordi's and Puccini's grief).

But Puccini began, as usual, to waver. He wrote Sybil on September 25, 1906, "I'm rather preoccupied about *Conchita* [this was to be the title of the opera]—or rather I'm feeling weaker on the subject! What frightens me is her character and then the plot of the play—and then all the characters seem to me unlovable, and that is a very bad thing on the stage." His vacillation won him an angry letter from Giulio Ricordi.

Distraction was in sight. In January 1907 Puccini traveled—with the always seasick Elvira—to New York, where there was to be a six-week season of his operas, including the Metropolitan premieres of *Manon Lescaut* and *Butterfly.* Both were an immense success. The *Manon* cast included the beautiful Lina Cavalieri, with whom Puccini apparently had

This rare turn-of-the-century photograph shows Puccini with his son Tonio (by the composer in a cap), Giuseppe Razzi, Elvira, Carlo Carignani (holding straw bowler) and Mrs. Carignani. Elvira's daughter, Fosca, sits in front of Carignani by her aunt, Ida Razzi, who holds her young son, Gastone

a brief fling; *Butterfly* starred Geraldine Farrar (whom Puccini disliked, in spite of her immense success in the part).

Puccini's feelings about New York were mixed. "I prefer London and Paris," he wrote his sister Ramelde. "Here life is horribly expensive. The dollars fly. . . ." But there were compensations. "How the women seek me out and want me! Even an old man like me. . . . *Ciao,* I'm going to bed; Elvira's there already, otherwise I wouldn't be writing what I've written. She Othello-izes as always, but I keep my nose clean. . . . Tear this up."

Before his departure for America, Puccini had met a friend, Marchese Piero Antinori, who had just returned from there. He advised the composer to see a current hit play, Belasco's *Girl of the Golden West.* Puccini took the advice, but his immediate reaction was not total enthusiasm. He wrote Tito Ricordi, "I've found some good hints in Belasco, but nothing definitive or solid or complete. The atmosphere of the Wild West attracts me, but in all the plays I have seen [he had also gone to two other Belasco hits, *The Music Master* and *Rose of the Rancho*] I found only good scenes here and there. Never a clear, simple line of development . . . and sometimes in very bad taste and old-hat."

From Paris, however, on his way home, he wrote to Belasco for a copy of the play. Sybil was enthusiastic about it and personally commissioned an Italian translation. Meanwhile, Illica had been put back to work on *Marie Antoinette;* so another librettist had to be found. It was Carlo Zangarini, librettist and also translator of librettos (including *Pelléas*). By August 1907 Puccini was enthusiastic, and he wrote to Giulio Ricordi, "This is it! *The Girl* promises to become a second *Bohème,* but stronger, bolder, vaster. I have an idea for a grand scene, a clearing in the California forest with colossal trees, but it requires eight or ten horses as supers."

At the piano of this room, in his villa at Torre del Lago,
Puccini wrote the score for Madama Butterfly. *His text was*
adapted from a play by David Belasco, which the composer had
seen in London. Though he understood little English, he had
been moved to tears, so clear and poignant was the plot

Confidence filled Puccini as he
rehearsed his cast—Giovanni
Zenatello, Rosina Storchio, Giuseppe
De Luca—for the premiere of Madama
Butterfly at La Scala (below). But
the night of February 17, 1904, proved
the blackest of his career, a fiasco
in which his music was drowned in a
sea of jeers. Three months later,
on May 28, 1904, the Teatro Grande
of Brescia gave a revised version
of the opera, and Puccini was
vindicated. His Pinkerton in Brescia
was also Zenatello, shown with
the Brescia Sharpless, Virgilio
Bellatti (right). The Cio-Cio-San,
Salomea Krusceniska (middle right),
later gathered with the full cast
for an official portrait (below right).
The Metropolitan Opera's most popular
performer of the title heroine was
Geraldine Farrar (below far right), who
sang in the company's 1907 premiere and
played the part ninety-five times.
In second place is Licia Albanese (far
right), whose first of forty-eight
geishas there was heard in 1940

alle prove di
" BUTTERFLY „

While waiting for the libretto to be finished, Puccini traveled some more: to Vienna, where *Butterfly* was given at the Hofoper; to Naples for the Italian premiere of *Salomé,* conducted by Strauss and, as Puccini wrote Ricordi, "sung (?) by Bellincioni, who dances marvelously. . . ." And then, from Naples, with Elvira for a holiday in Egypt. Both hated it, though Puccini amused himself with a new gadget: a camera.

In the same letter to Ricordi, Puccini wrote, "I am reading *La Fanciulla* and I find that Zangarini has done well; naturally some points, both scenic and literary, must be corrected, and I'll write my remarks in the margin. I am already savoring the moment when I will finally go to work."

Zangarini's work on the libretto soon aroused more than marginal remarks from Puccini, and—much against Zangarini's will—he was given

The Metropolitan Opera staged a new production of Madama Butterfly *in 1958. Below is Act I, the heroine's entrance with Theodor Uppman (Sharpless), Barry Morell (Pinkerton) and Teresa Stratas (Cio-Cio-San). At left is Act II, the humming chorus, with Stratas and Nedda Casei (Suzuki)*

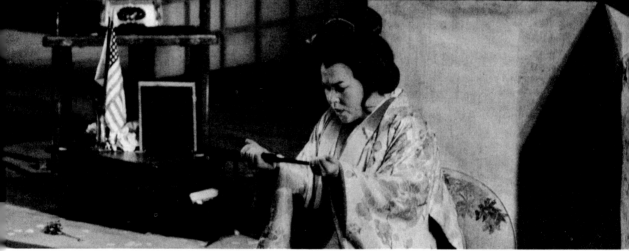

a collaborator, Guelfo Civinini. But the collaboration lacked an essential element: Giulio Ricordi, in poor health, was in semi-retirement, unable to intervene in the disputes between composer and writers. The libretto limped on, as Puccini wrote Sybil: *"The Girl* is more difficult than I thought. . . . For the time being I have lost my way."

In the autumn of 1908, however, he was beginning to score the opera. After a visit from Toscanini and Gatti-Casazza, newly appointed artistic director and general manager of the Metropolitan, it was decided that this American story would have its world premiere at America's leading opera house, then engaged in a battle with the adventurous Hammerstein company and hence eager to score such a coup.

But then work suffered a tragic interruption.

Vulnerable heroines caught in believable human tragedies drew from Puccini music of overpowering emotion. At left, Renata Scotto as Cio-Cio-San bids her child farewell, then commits suicide. Below, not Pinkerton and Trouble but Puccini with his step-granddaughter Biki—set to sail on his yacht, the Cio-Cio-San

Elvira was not the sort of housekeeper who is good with servants (though she was herself a good cook). So the Torre del Lago establishment was chronically short of help. During Puccini's convalescence after his automobile accident, a village girl, Doria Manfredi, plain but devoted, was hired to lend a hand in taking care of the invalid. She proved indispensable, and as Giacomo wrote, on coming back from America, "There's nobody to wait on table, and no cook—Doria has to do everything."

Among her chores was the ironing, which she sometimes did in the late evening, after dinner. One night Elvira came down to the study and found Puccini and Doria talking by the door to the garden. Elvira began to scream insults at the girl, and when Doria ran and locked herself in her room, Elvira followed her and pounded on the door for hours.

The next morning the girl fled to her home, half-dead with fright. Elvira made threats all over the village, calling the girl a whore. Needless to say, the villagers, all well aware of Puccini's peccadilloes (and his penchant for servant girls), believed Elvira. The desperate Doria took

Puccini sought stimulation in travel. Once he was nearly killed when his car plunged into a steep ditch, leaving him in a wheelchair. He visited Egypt once (right) and England often. In London he met the beautiful Sybil Seligman, who was to become his lifetime friend

Touring Club Italiano

14, Via Monte Napoleone - MILANO - Via Monte Napoleone, 14

Case pour la photographie de la voiture.

PERMIS
DE
LIBRE
Circulation
Internationale

N° 118

délivré le 9 Settan 1906, sous le n° 118

à Monsieur Giacomo Puccini

membre de la Société, demeurant à Milano

rue Giuseppe Verdi, n° 4

Le Directeur Général du T. C. I.

Le Titulaire du permis

poison and died after five days of atrocious suffering, continuing to declare her innocence. The Puccinis separated: the horrified Giacomo to Rome with his friends the Tostis, the unrepentant Elvira to Milan. The Manfredi family decided to sue her; the local doctor performed an autopsy and proved that Doria was a virgin.

For four months Giacomo and Elvira lived apart. She was determined to defend herself in court. Giacomo tried to work, with two of his sisters taking care of him; but the atmosphere at Torre—where he was

David Belasco (left), wizard of the American theater, wrote The Girl of the Golden West, *which Puccini adapted on commission from the Metropolitan Opera. After the premiere in New York, the maestro sailed home on the* Lusitania, *posing first with the captain, Tito Ricordi and son Tonio, then on deck with Ricordi*

besieged by reporters—was intolerable. Tonio, who had sided with his mother, in his distress went first to Munich and then threatened to leave for Africa, to start a new life there.

This threat, more than anything else, brought about a meeting—after almost four months—between Tonio's parents. But it ended in recriminations. Elvira insisted on continuing her disastrous legal course. The case was tried, she lost, was sentenced to five months' imprisonment, a fine of 700 lire and payment of costs. Finally, Giacomo persuaded the Manfredis to accept a settlement, and the lawsuit was dropped. In September 1909 Giacomo, Elvira and Tonio were all back at Torre. On the 30th of that month Puccini wrote Sybil, "I'm working hard: *The Girl* goes well and I've nearly finished the second act—where there's a love duet that seems to me to have come out well. . . . In my home I have peace—Elvira is good—and the three of us live happily together."

Interrupted by the usual trips to see his operas performed—*Butterfly* in Brussels, *Manon Lescaut* in Paris (where it had to contend with, and overcome, a nationalistic admiration for the Massenet version of the story)—work continued on the new opera until August 15, when Puccini wrote Sybil, "*The Girl* is finished at last! . . . *The Girl* has come out, in my opinion, the best opera I have written."

Early in November Puccini, this time with Tonio and not with Elvira (for whom one taste of New York was enough), sailed on the *George Washington* for America. "Here I am at sea; we have an apartment known as the Imperial Suite," he wrote Ricordi. "Bath, bedroom, sitting room with soft divans . . . dining room with furniture in very refined English taste, ingenious closets even with lights inside. . . ."

New York was agog, and Gatti-Casazza (with Otto Kahn enthusiastically and munificently backing him) was preparing things in style. The cast was first-rate: Caruso, Emmy Destinn as *la girl*, Pasquale Amato. Toscanini —whose conducting of a *Manon Lescaut* revival at La Scala had strength-

The premiere of La Fanciulla del West, *on December 10, 1910, was the event of New York's musical season. Toscanini conducted, and at the end of Act II Emmy Destinn (Minnie) cheated Pasquale Amato (Jack Rance) at poker to save the life of Enrico Caruso (the bandit Ramerrez, alias Dick Johnson)*

85

Hello!

Enrico Caruso waited many years to create
a Puccini role, and Ramerrez gave him
the golden opportunity; on a photo of himself
as the bandit, he wrote the opera's opening word,
"Hello!" The most famous photo from
the premiere is the hanging scene,
with Destinn and Caruso pitted against
Amato and the miners

ened Puccini's affection for him—was in charge, and Tito Ricordi would stage the opera in collaboration with the great Belasco himself.

The weather was vile. But despite snow and cold, and despite raised prices (increased still further by scalpers), a capacity audience filled the Met. Their applause rocked the rafters. The critics were generally respectful, though Richard Aldrich in *The New York Times* said the piece lacked the "melodic luster, outline, point and fluency" of earlier works by the composer. He noticed the influence of Debussy (which would become more

*As westerns became a cliché at the movies, the originality
and flavor of* La Fanciulla del West *were obscured.
Among the artists who have reminded the public of* Fanciulla's
*worth are Maria Jeritza and Lawrence Tibbett, paired as
Minnie and Rance in the Met's 1929 revival (above).
Dorothy Kirsten (right) did the role in 1961, with
Richard Tucker as Ramerrez, garbed in the suede jacket
Caruso had worn at the world premiere*

marked in later Puccini music) and of Strauss. Other critics—including Lawrence Gilman in *Harper's Weekly*—also mentioned these alien influences.

But Puccini was content. From the *Lusitania,* on the way home, he wrote a friend, "At the third performance more than 1,000 people were turned away. . . . The musical performance was magnificent and the *mise en scène* amazing. Caruso great, Amato excellent, Toscanini immense and good, a real angel."

VI

WAR AND PEACE

I N the evening of June 5, 1912, Giulio Ricordi—who was a composer in his spare time, under the pen name of J. Burgmein—sat down at his desk to correct a piece of music. He was found there the next morning, dead, a pencil clenched in his hand.

Puccini heard the news in Munich, where he wrote to Sybil, "You simply can't imagine how grieved I am at his death." He had more than one reason to grieve. To the fatherless Giacomo, Ricordi had long been a paternal figure, at times severe (the older, happily married man particularly disapproved of the composer's constant wild oats) but always concerned, ready with advice and help. It was, after all, Giulio Ricordi who had first recognized Puccini's worth, on the frail evidence of *Le Villi* (first version), and had sustained him through adversity. Now the firm

The Metropolitan Opera's 1969-70 revival of La Fanciulla del West *offered a new Girl, Renata Tebaldi, shown here with Andrea Velis as Joe. The soprano made her entrance by shooting a pistol from a miner's hand, then delivered one of the primmest, sweetest, most innocent Minnies in the company's history*

would be in the hands of Tito, Giulio's difficult son, whose attitude toward Puccini was—perhaps out of jealousy—cold, at times even hostile.

For Puccini a period of confusion began. Always, when one opera was launched, he floundered for a while before really getting down to another. But this time it was worse. He seemed to grope in all directions, including several already tried and discarded: he revived the notion of the *Florentine Tragedy* and put Illica to work on it, he had another meeting with D'Annunzio. He set a new young friend, Giuseppe Adami, to reading Heine and Dickens. And his own gloom deepened. From Milan, early in 1913, he wrote Elvira, "I have no libretto. I have no work. My publisher is my enemy."

At about this time he returned to another old idea, one Ricordi had disliked: a trio of one-act operas. Hearing of a highly successful Grand Guignol play by Didier Gold, *La Houppelande* (The Cloak), he rushed off to Paris to see it. He asked Tito to acquire the rights, and he entrusted the libretto-making first to an old friend, the diplomat and writer Ferdinando Martini, and then, when Martini bowed out, to the young Giuseppe Adami, who was to become the companion of Puccini's last years and an early (and inaccurate) biographer.

The other two panels of this Triptych—as it came to be called—were missing, and Puccini turned to other ideas, notably a story by Ouida, "Two Little Wooden Shoes," which later became the Mascagni opera *Lodoletta*. Puccini also visited Vienna for a *Tosca* with the young Moravian soprano Maria Jeritza. It was a superlative performance, and the beautiful artist was to set a standard for the role that in Puccini's estimation no other would equal. She also, by accident, established the practice (not always observed by her successors) of singing "Vissi d'arte" prostrate. The baritone had involuntarily knocked her down, and rather than struggle to her feet during the aria she delivered it—memorably—from where she lay.

World War I shifted the opening of La Rondine *from Vienna to Monaco's ornate Casino theater, on March 27, 1917. There Gilda Dalla Rizza and Tito Schipa rehearsed the romantic leads. Some lauded the score's "charm and freshness," but Tito Ricordi said "bad Lehár" and refused to publish it*

In Vienna, Puccini saw again the impresarios of the Carltheatre, who on a previous Viennese visit had approached him with the invitation to write an operetta. A great admirer of Lehár, Puccini was intrigued, but the libretto offered was too silly for consideration. They now promised him a new text, which was eventually produced: *La Rondine*. Adami, who had more or less finished *Il Tabarro* (though Puccini hadn't set to work on it, in the absence of the other two texts), was commissioned to make a translation. Again Puccini waxed hot and cold about the subject, and Adami—who lacked the authority of Giacosa and the theatrical skill of Illica—could do little to satisfy him, until he finally made an obvious but fertile suggestion: turn the wispy operetta into a real opera. Puccini became excited and fell to work.

The story of *La Rondine* also involves Puccini's relations with his publisher. Tito was openly pushing a young discovery of his, Riccardo Zandonai, and made no secret of his antagonism for the older composer. When Puccini told him of the Viennese project Tito was skeptical. In the end he turned it down, and Puccini took it to the rival firm Sonzogno (whose competition *Le Villi* had notoriously failed to win decades before).

Work progressed simultaneously on *Il Tabarro* and *La Rondine,* but they were composed under the terrible shadow of the First World War. Italy, at the beginning, was neutral, and Puccini was the most neutral of Italians. Personally he liked Austria and disliked France, and as the least political-minded of men he felt and displayed an indifference to the fate of Europe which shocked and enraged some of his associates, especially Toscanini, who finally stopped speaking to his long-time friend. Toscanini's low opinion of *Butterfly* (of which Puccini was well aware) contributed to the breach, painful for all.

La Rondine was fully orchestrated by the spring of 1916; early the following year a friend of Adami's, the young playwright Giovacchino

La Rondine lingered at the Metropolitan Opera between 1928 and 1936 because Lucrezia Bori brought the needed fragile grace to Magda and Beniamino Gigli, her original co-star, could offer honeyed tones as Ruggero. But after Bori retired, La Rondine *was never to return to the repertory*

Forzano, spoke to Puccini about a one-act play of his, a story set in a convent. Puccini—whose sister Iginia was now Mother Superior of a little convent near Lucca—immediately became interested. The libretto was quickly drafted.

Meanwhile, at a secret meeting in Switzerland with the Viennese impresarios, Puccini had persuaded them to renounce their right to a Vienna premiere of *La Rondine,* which was given instead in one of the few neutral spots left on the continent: Monte Carlo, on May 4, 1917. In the jewel-like Théâtre du Casino it was mounted by Raoul Gunsbourg with no expense spared. The cast was headed by Gilda Dalla Rizza and Tito Schipa, who sang to the glittering audience (including the composer, Elvira and Fosca), enchanting it. The *Journal de Monaco* reported a total success and called *La Rondine* "une comédie musicale variée, vivante . . . exquise."

While Puccini was at Monte Carlo, Forzano was at work on another libretto to complete the trio: *Gianni Schicchi,* thus incidentally fulfilling a long-cherished ambition of Puccini's, to write a comic opera. By June the text was ready, and on October 17, 1917, Puccini could write a friend, "I am totally at work on *Gianni Schicchi.* For the moment I can think of nothing else. . . ."

Finally the war ended, and with it some of Puccini's private concerns (chief among them the safety of Tonio, who had been at the front). It was time to think of the *Trittico*'s premiere, which had been awarded to the Metropolitan, not with Toscanini this time but with the conductor Roberto Moranzoni, who came to Italy to go over the music with the composer.

Puccini was unable to attend the gala premiere on December 14, 1918. Ocean travel was still risky because of floating mines, and state-rooms and visas were hard to get. Gatti-Casazza had of course assembled a starry cast, with Claudia Muzio in *Il Tabarro,* Geraldine Farrar as Suor Angelica and Giuseppe De Luca and Florence Easton in *Schicchi,* which was—as it long remained—the one real success of the triple bill.

The Italian premiere, at the Costanzi in Rome on January 11, 1919, concerned Puccini even more. There the conductor was Gino Marinuzzi, and the array of stars included Carlo Galeffi, Maria Labia and the tenor Edward Johnson (or, as he was then known, Edoardo di Giovanni) in *Il Tabarro,* Gilda Dalla Rizza in *Suor Angelica* and also in *Schicchi,* where Galeffi sang the title role. Again the press singled out the comic opera for praise, expressing grave reservations about the other two works. Toscanini, in the audience, cut Puccini dead, and when asked his opinion of *Il Tabarro* said, "I don't like it at all." Naturally, this opinion was promptly reported back to the composer, widening the rift.

Still, the Costanzi's box office was doing exceptional business, and Puccini, probably hoping that once again—as with *Tosca* and *Butterfly*—the public would confound the critics, came back to Torre in good humor. He had only one little chore to do: write an "Inno a Roma," to celebrate Italian victory. It was requested by the mayor of Rome, Prince Colonna, and Puccini, sensitive both to officialdom and to the aristocracy, hastened to comply, though he privately considered the piece worthless. Later, after his death, it was taken up by the Mussolini regime, giving Puccini the posthumous and undeserved denomination of Fascist.

VII

TURANDOT AND THE END

O<small>N</small> June 1919, Puccini managed to pay a first postwar visit to London and the Seligmans. Sybil's son Vincent, years later, described the composer at that time: "He seemed to have changed but little during the long interval since we had seen him last; his hair had begun to turn white, but it was as abundant as ever; his movements were perhaps a little slower and more measured, but the oncoming of old age over which he continually lamented in his letters was with him a very gradual and almost imperceptible process, and no one would have guessed he had turned sixty; he looked, as he always did until a few months before his death, the very picture of health."

Others, notably Mario Gallati, the proprietor of the Ivy Restaurant (quoted in Stanley Jackson's *Monsieur Butterfly*), found him very differ-

Melancholy often swept Puccini as he contemplated Lake Massaciuccoli at Torre del Lago. He was growing old, his wife's temper gnawed at his nerves, war made work uncertain. In despair he wrote, "My solitude is vast like the sea, flat as the surface of a lake, black like night, green like bile"

ent: "It was obviously an effort for him to get up from the table, and he seemed to have aged."

Whether he looked aged or not, Puccini certainly felt older. For some time he had taken to dyeing his hair, and he was interested in various "rejuvenation" cures, including the famous "monkey-gland" treatment of Dr. Voronoff, which he was dissuaded from taking only because his doctors insisted it would adversely affect his diabetes. With age, and with a kind of philosophical melancholy, Puccini had also acquired a certain resignation: he and Elvira got on much better, he had made peace with Leoncavallo before the other composer's death, and his feelings about Tito Ricordi—now that his mistaken expenditures had brought on his dismissal from the family firm—grew almost affectionate.

Among his sorrows of the time there was an enforced move. At Torre del Lago, during the war and the fuel shortage, a peat factory had been set up. It was noisy and smelly, and there seemed no sign of its being dismantled. Puccini had bought, some time before, a piece of land on the outskirts of Viareggio, set back from the sea, with a number of tall pine trees. There he had a villa constructed to his special requirements, and he moved into it at the end of December 1921. He never sold the house at Torre, visiting it occasionally and using it as a base for shooting. But for the rest of his life his real home was the new villa, which he fitted out with every sort of gadget, including a radio. The house was looted during World War II; none of Puccini's belongings remain there now. The pines are dying from the fumes of traffic, and the place has a gloominess that must have been there in Puccini's time. But it was in that dark villa that he wrote most of *Turandot*.

It began the previous March when Puccini was lunching in Milan with Adami and Renato Simoni, critic and playwright. Some time earlier Puccini had set them to preparing a libretto based on a Dickens subject.

Visitors to Puccini's villa at Torre del Lago can see his hunting gear lined up as though the owner might appear at any moment to put it back into use. An abundance of pheasant and waterfowl on Lake Massaciuccoli provided diversion for the composer whenever he could flee his work

METROPOLITAN OPERA HOUSE

SATURDAY EVENING, DECEMBER 14TH, AT 8 O'CLOCK
FIRST PERFORMANCE ON ANY STAGE
GIACOMO PUCCINI'S

THREE ONE-ACT OPERAS

I.

IL TABARRO

(THE CLOAK)

Book by GIUSEPPE ADAMI after "La Houppelande," by Didier Gold

MICHELE	LUIGI MONTESANTO	GIORGETTA	CLAUDIA MUZIO
LUIGI	GIULIO CRIMI	LA FRUGOLA	ALICE GENTLE
IL TINCA	ANGELO BADA	VENDITORE DI CANZONI	PIETRO AUDISIO
IL TALPA	ADAMO DIDUR	L'INNAMORATA	MARIE TIFFANY

CARRIERS, MIDINETTES, AN ORGAN-GRINDER.

SCENE:—THE SEINE, PARIS. MICHELE'S BARGE.
Painted by Ernest M. Gros after a sketch by Pietro Stroppa.

II.

SUOR ANGELICA

(SISTER ANGELICA)

Book by GIOACHINO FORZANO

SUOR ANGELICA	GERALDINE FARRAR	SUOR DOLCINA	MARIE MATTFELD
LA ZIA PRINCIPESSA	FLORA PERINI	SORELLE CERCATRICI {	KITTY BEALE
LA BADESSA	RITA FORNIA		MINNIE EGENER
LA SUOR ZELATRICE	MARIE SUNDELIUS	LE CONVERSE {	MARIE TIFFANY
LA MAESTRA DELLE NOVIZIE	CECIL ARDEN		VERA WARWICK
SUOR GENOVIEFFA	MARY ELLIS	UNA NOVIZIA	PHILLIS WHITE
SUOR OSMINA	MARGUERITE BELLERI		

SCENE:—A CONVENT IN ITALY. END OF 1600.
Painted by Frank Platzer after a sketch by Pietro Stroppa.

III.

GIANNI SCHICCHI

Book by GIOACHINO FORZANO

GIANNI SCHICCHI	GIUSEPPE DE LUCA	SIMONE	ADAMO DIDUR
LAURETTA	FLORENCE EASTON	MARCO	LOUIS D'ANGELO
LA VECCHIA	KATHLEEN HOWARD	LA CIESCA	MARIE SUNDELIUS
RINUCCIO	GIULIO CRIMI	SPINELLOCCIO	POMPILIO MALATESTA
GHERARDO	ANGELO BADA	SER AMANTIO DI NICOLAO	ANDRES DE SEGUROLA
NELLA	MARIE TIFFANY	PINELLINO	VINCENZO RESCHIGLIAN
GHERARDINO	MARIO MALATESTA	GUCCIO	CARL SCHLEGEL
BETTO	PAOLO ANANIAN		

SCENE:—THE BEDROOM OF THE LATE BUOSO DONATI. (FLORENCE ANNO 1299.)
Painted by Pieretto Bianco after a sketch by Galileo Chini, Florence.

CONDUCTOR, ROBERTO MORANZONI

STAGE DIRECTOR	RICHARD ORDYNSKI
CHORUS MASTER	GIULIO SETTI

TECHNICAL DIRECTOR	EDWARD SIEDLE
STAGE MANAGER	ARMANDO AGNINI

Costumes executed by Mme. Louise Musaeus.
Properties and accessories by the Siedle Studio.

Giulio Gatti-Casazza, the manager of La Scala at the time of the first Madama Butterfly, ran the Metropolitan Opera from 1908 to 1935. During his tenure he secured two Puccini premieres, La Fanciulla del West and a trio of one-act works, Il Trittico.

Puccini found an able colleague in Giovacchino Forzano, who provided the words for two parts of Il Trittico—Suor Angelica *and* Gianni Schicchi. *A former singer, the librettist also wrote texts for Leoncavallo and Mascagni and was to stage the world premiere of Puccini's last opera,* Turandot

Then he had grown cold on the project, and the lunch was apparently intended to pacify the rightly annoyed authors. In the course of the meal, someone (accounts differ) brought up Carlo Gozzi, the eighteenth-century Venetian dramatist, and his fairy-tale play *Turandotte,* which Puccini may well have known about, since his old teacher Bazzini had written an opera on it, and more recently (in 1917) so had Ferruccio Busoni. In any case, Simoni owned an Italian translation of the Schiller adaptation of the work. He telephoned home and had it brought to the restaurant so Puccini could read it on the train.

Puccini, from Rome, wrote Simoni, "I have read *Turandot.* It seems to me advisable to adhere closely to the story. Yesterday I spoke with a

The world premiere of Il Tabarro *at the Metropolitan Opera in 1918 starred Luigi Montesanto as Michele, Claudia Muzio as his wife, Giorgetta, and Giulio Crimi as her lover, Michele (below). Shown right is the company's 1977 revival with Hildegard Behrens (Giorgetta), Gianfranco Cecchele (Luigi), Cornell MacNeil (Michele)*

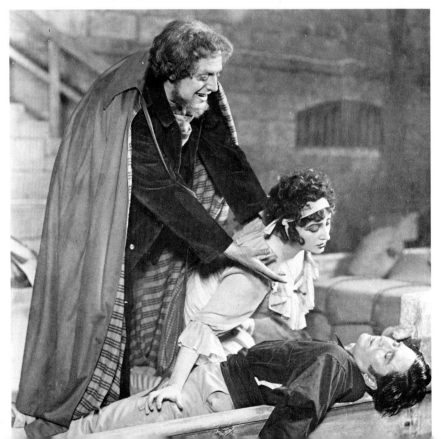

foreign lady who told me how this work was given in Germany, staged by Max Reinhardt. . . . Simplify it as far as the number of acts is concerned and work to make it trim, effective, and above all exalt Turandot's amorous passion, which she has stifled for so long beneath the ashes of her great pride. . . . Finally: a Turandot through the modern mind, yours, Adami's and mine."

The word *modern* is significant. Clearly Puccini, with this libretto, wanted to get away from what was being considered the "typical" Puccini opera, with a frail heroine and lovely tunes. Alert to developments in contemporary music, he not only attended Strauss and Debussy premieres

Suor Angelica pays tribute to Puccini's sister Iginia (above), who took religious vows to become Sister Giulia Enrichetta and who was Mother Superior to the convent at Vicopelago. At the Met premiere in 1918, Geraldine Farrar (right) created the title role, which was sung in 1976 by Gilda Cruz-Romo (far right)

but was also aware of Stravinsky and Schoenberg (before his death he went to the Italian premiere of *Pierrot Lunaire* in Florence and met the Viennese composer). *Turandot* was to be a new opera in every sense.

The project began to take shape. During the summer of 1920, librettists and composer met in the hills of Bagni di Lucca for further discussion, and Puccini also picked the brains of a friend and old China hand, Baron Fassini, who lent him a Chinese music box. Some of its tunes found their way into the opera.

Gianni Schicchi is Puccini's wry homage to his Tuscan heritage. The original cast at the Met in 1918 offered Florence Easton as Lauretta, Giulio Crimi as Rinuccio and Giuseppe De Luca as Schicchi (above). A 1975 production (right) offered Judith Blegen as Lauretta, Frank Guarrera as Schicchi, Irene Dalis as Zita

In Puccini's letters of 1922, optimism and depression alternate. At times *Turandot* languishes, and he thinks of other projects: a *Cagliostro,* for example. Then he has bursts of energy and inspiration and, as usual, suggestions for his librettists. In November (after almost two years of work), he decided Liù had to die. "Make her die under torture. Why not?" he wrote Adami. "Her death could help soften the heart of the princess."

On February 1, 1923, the thirtieth anniversary of the premiere of *Manon Lescaut,* Toscanini conducted a triumphant revival of the work at La Scala. The next day Puccini wrote the conductor, "You have given me the greatest satisfaction of my life. *Manon* in your interpretation surpasses everything I conceived in those far-off times. . . . Last night I felt all your great soul and your love for your old friend and comrade of the early days." The reconciliation was complete, and now Toscanini was to be in charge of *Turandot* as it moved toward completion.

By March 1924 Puccini had finished and orchestrated the whole opera through the scene of Liù's death. Only fifteen minutes of music remained to be written, but there was trouble over the definitive wording of the great love duet that was to be the opera's culmination, its crowning moment. Finally Simoni and Adami supplied the verses, on September 1, 1924, and Puccini immediately began jotting down sketches, scrawling reminders to himself in the margins. On one sheet he wrote, "Find here the characteristic, lovely, unusual melody."

Interrupting the search for that melody, on October 26, 1924, he paid a visit to the town of Celle, the home of his remote ancestors. It was a sentimental visit, one he had been promising for twenty years. Official photographs were taken outside the ancestral home. In them Puccini looks aged, drawn. And, in fact, his health was poor. For months he had been troubled by a bad cough—with sore throats, a long-recurring

Beverly Sills is one of the few sopranos to have performed the soprano leads in all three operas of Il Trittico *during a single evening, at the New York City Opera in 1967. Here she broods as Giorgetta in* Il Tabarro, *romances as Lauretta with Rinuccio in* Gianni Schicchi, *grieves as Suor Angelica*

*It is only a short drive from Torre del Lago to the Mediterranean,
where the Cio-Cio-San lay at anchor. Sometimes Tito Ricordi
would spell Puccini at the wheel (top). Cars, boats—
and at right, with Tonio in Viareggio, a motorcycle. Speed
and mechanical locomotion were irresistible to Puccini*

complaint of his—and after long delay he went to a doctor. A growth was found at the base of the larynx. At Tonio's insistence there were further examinations. The tumor was malignant and too far advanced to be operated on. The only possible treatment was radium therapy at the Ledoux clinic, Brussels.

Neither Puccini nor Elvira was told the true situation. But Puccini had some forebodings. Toscanini (aware of the reality) came to Viareggio to see him off, and Puccini whispered to him, "If anything happens to me, don't abandon my *Turandot*."

At first the Brussels treatment seemed promising. Puccini actually attended a performance of his beloved *Butterfly*. But then the excruciating

Renato Simoni and Giuseppe Adami, shown above with Puccini, were the librettists for the composer's final opera, Turandot. *On October 26, 1924, during the composition of* Turandot, *Puccini made a nostalgic visit to the home of his ancestors at Celle. Here the great man was surrounded by family, friends and admirers, who posed with him.*

radioactive needles were inserted into the tumor, and the composer had to be fed nasally. Unable to speak, he scrawled messages on a pad. Tonio and Fosca took turns at his bedside (Elvira, ill herself with bronchitis, had remained in Milan), writing optimistic reports. The treatment seemed effective, and the doctor released a statement: "Puccini en sortira." At 4 P.M. on Friday, November 28, Fosca was writing to Sybil: "Everything is going well, and the doctors are more than satisfied; our adored Papa is saved!"

Before finishing the letter, she left the room to look for Sybil's address. The nurse called her back a moment later. Puccini had collapsed. A heart attack. The needles were removed from his throat. At four in the

morning on Saturday, he whispered to Fosca a few words about her mother (they have been variously reported, but his last thought was Elvira), then died.

For Puccini, death was not the end. He had left the almost-finished *Turandot* behind him, and Toscanini—true to his word—did not abandon it. For completion of the last act the conductor gave Puccini's notes and sketches to Franco Alfano, the successful composer of works like *Risur-rezione* (1904) and *La Leggenda di Sakuntala* (1921). Alfano performed

In 1922, with heavy heart, Puccini had moved from Torre del Lago down the tree-lined road to Viareggio. Odor and noise from fuel factories had ruined his sanctuary. In his somber new home (below), as he wrote Turandot, *Elvira saw his health decline. After an operation, unable to speak, he scribbled his last words, "Elvira, poor, sad woman"*

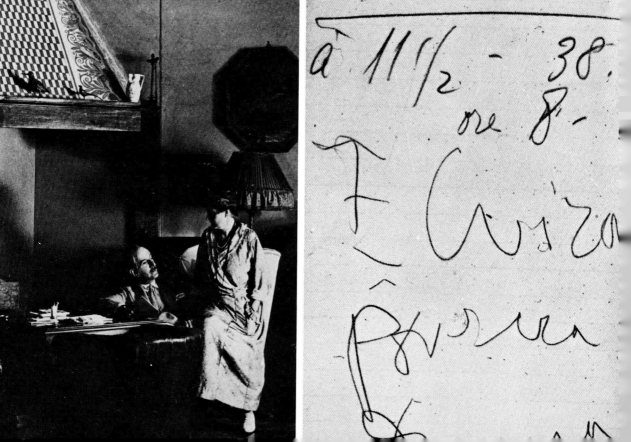

Death claimed Puccini on November 29, 1924, at Brussels' Institut
de la Couronne, where he had begun painful radium therapy for
cancer of the throat. After a Requiem was said at the Church of
Sainte-Marie, a cortège moved on to a train that took his remains
to Italy and final rest in a mausoleum in his villa at Torre del Lago

Since only rough drafts existed for the Turandot *finale, Arturo Toscanini chose composer Franco Alfano (bottom right) to collate them. Rosa Raisa (below) created the title role at the premiere, at La Scala in 1926, but Toscanini stopped conducting after Liù's suicide, telling the public, "Here the master put down his pen"*

the thankless job tactfully, under Toscanini's supervision. The conductor also took care about the sets and costumes (which had been already under way before Puccini's trip to Brussels) and the casting.

Turandot finally opened at La Scala on April 25, 1926, almost a year and a half after the composer's death. Alfano's contribution, on the first night, was not heard. After the death of Liù, Toscanini, overcome with emotion, stopped the orchestra and said, "At this point the master laid down his pen."

Turandot *arrived at the Metropolitan Opera on November 16, 1926, with Maria Jeritza in the title role; below she links arms with manager Giulio Gatti-Casazza and conductor Tullio Serafin. Her Calaf was Giacomo Lauri-Volpi (bottom). At right, Birgit Nilsson in La Scala's spectacular 1958 staging designed by Nicola Benois*

Expectedly, the opera was a success. But then, like Verdi's swan-song *Falstaff*, its popularity waned for a while. It is only in recent years that the strange, even revolutionary *Turandot* has returned firmly to the international repertory, from which its popular predecessors—*Bohème, Butterfly, Tosca*—have never departed.

Turandot became a favorite in the Metropolitan Opera's repertory in 1961 with a new production by designer Cecil Beaton. At left, Pang, Pong and Ping (Robert Nagy, Charles Anthony, Frank Guarrera) and Timur mourning Liù's death (Bonaldo Giaiotti, Teresa Stratas). Above, Montserrat Caballé as Turandot, Franco Corelli as Calaf

THE PUCCINI REPERTORY

STORIES OF THE OPERAS

Compiled by Stephen Wadsworth

LE VILLI

ACT I. In a clearing in the Black Forest, mountaineers and villagers gather to celebrate the betrothal of Roberto to Anna, daughter of Guglielmo Wulf. Roberto is dressed for travel, headed for Mainz, where he will claim an inheritance left him by an elderly female relative. Anna approaches to bid him farewell, offering him a bouquet of forget-me-nots with the hope that their name will hold true. Roberto asks only for a smile, but Anna feels sad, disturbed by a presentiment that she will never again see him. He reassures her: "Doubt your God, but never doubt my love." Roberto asks for a blessing from Guglielmo, who responds with a prayer for his safety; everyone joins in. Roberto now takes leave of Anna, turning at the bridge to wave.

125

Statue of Puccini at Torre del Lago

A narrative introduces an intermezzo depicting Roberto's seduction by a loose woman in Mainz and his betrayal of Anna, who, forgotten, pines away for him. She dies in winter.

A second intermezzo represents the witches' sabbath, when the Wilis, spirits of girls who have died for love, wait to ensnare their betrayers and dance them to death.

ACT II. On his doorstep, Guglielmo bemoans his daughter's passing, wishing the Wilis' revenge on Roberto. When he retires, the Wilis warn Anna of Roberto's approach. He comes to Guglielmo's house, filled with anguished reminiscences and wondering if Anna might still live, but a strange force stays his hand from knocking. Hearing Anna's voice, he turns and sees her on the bridge. "I am no longer love," she warns—"I am revenge." She castigates him, then draws him into the merciless dance, from which he cannot escape. He soon collapses, exhausted, at Anna's feet; triumphantly, she calls him her own as the Wilis and spirits cry hosannahs.

EDGAR

ACT I. On a Sunday in spring in a small Flemish town (c. 1302), the gentle Fidelia greets the dawn and then Edgar, whom she loves. Edgar loves her in return, but is also smitten with the gypsy girl Tigrana, whom Fidelia's family raised from infancy. Now Tigrana accosts Edgar passionately. When she starts to leave, she is stopped by Fidelia's brother Frank, who loves her unrequitedly. Tigrana scorns him sarcastically, and as the congregation issues from the church, she goads the crowd with an irreverent song.

When they revile her, Edgar steps forth in her defense, deciding to flee with her for a life of lust. Impulsively he sets his house on fire, and the two take flight, only to be intercepted by the jealous Frank, who presses Edgar to duel. The ensuing scuffle, in which Frank is wounded, attracts the townspeople, who abhor the behavior of the escaping couple.

ACT II. Some time later, Edgar, a guest at a palace orgy, bursts onto a moonlit terrace, declining the pleasures offered him within. His thoughts are with Fidelia, the sweet vision he deserted for a vagrant life with a gypsy woman. When Tigrana herself approaches seductively, Edgar rejects her, but she reminds him that he abandoned everything for her: without her he can only be a beggar. When a military fanfare interrupts them, Edgar is inspired to join the troops, thereby escaping the gypsy's thrall. The captain happens to be Frank, to whom Edgar confesses his guilt and suffering, imploring his old enemy to accept him into the ranks. Frank, whose love for Tigrana has turned to loathing, ignores her plea to leave her lover behind and admits Edgar into his company. As the soldiers leave, exalting the fatherland, the disconsolate Tigrana swears vengeance.

ACT III. The soldier Edgar has been reported dead in battle, and in a bastion near Courtrai a Requiem Mass is intoned for him. A monk speaks out against Edgar, enumerating his sins, but the forgiving Fidelia protests eloquently in her lover's favor. When Tigrana appears, the monk, joined by Frank, attempts to bribe her with pearls to denounce the dead man. She cooperates, condemning Edgar for treason. The angry soldiers begin to dismantle Edgar's coffin, meaning to throw his corpse to the birds. Now the monk uncloaks himself—it is Edgar, who now knows that it is Fidelia who loves him truly. Fidelia, overwhelmed with joy, races to his side but is stabbed by the vengeful Tigrana, whom the soldiers apprehend while Edgar bends despairingly over the body of his true, innocent love.

MANON LESCAUT

ACT I. Outside a bustling inn at Amiens, about 1721, Edmondo, his fellow-students and their sweethearts amuse themselves. When the Chevalier des Grieux appears, they taunt the youth for his lack of success in love; but he is a cynic on the subject and retorts with a teasing serenade to the girls. Soon the courtyard stirs with the arrival of a carriage bearing Manon and her brother, Lescaut, who is escorting the girl to a convent at their father's orders. Sharing the coach with them is the elderly Geronte, a wealthy Parisian gallant. As Manon alights, Des Grieux's cynicism melts away; while the innkeeper shows Lescaut and Geronte to their quarters, he passionately introduces himself to the girl. But she is called away by her brother, promising to return when night falls. The Chevalier rhapsodizes on her beauty to the amusement of the students. Geronte, encouraged by Lescaut's worldly ambitions for Manon, bribes the innkeeper to arrange for her abduction; overhearing the plan, Edmondo warns Des Grieux. As evening falls, Manon keeps her tryst with the Chevalier, who soon persuades her to escape both the convent and her elderly admirer by running off to Paris with him instead. Geronte returns to find the young lovers escaping in the carriage he had hired for himself and Manon; furious, he is calmed by the tipsy Lescaut, who assures him that a girl who loves luxury so much will be easily lured away from a poor student. As the other young people make a laughingstock of the old roué, he goes in to supper with Lescaut.

ACT II. True to Lescaut's prediction, Manon has abandoned her lover and is installed in a sumptuous Paris apartment provided, with the jewels she always dreamed of, by Geronte. When Lescaut calls to congratulate her on her success, she replies pensively that it cannot make up for the loss of Des Grieux, whom Lescaut has launched on a gambling career. In all this luxury, she says, there is a mortal chill. Manon's discontent is not relieved by five musicians singing a madrigal composed by Geronte, but her vanity is aroused when some of her sponsor's friends call to pay tribute to her glamour. Geronte joins them in watching the girl's dancing lesson, and she concludes the entertainment by singing a love song to the strains of a minuet. When her admirers leave, Manon is confronted by Des Grieux, obligingly summoned by Lescaut to ease her boredom. At first reproaching Manon as faithless, Des Grieux soon gives in to her beauty and her insistent declarations of true love. Just as the two embrace, Geronte surprises them; when Manon mocks his age, he leaves in a rage, hinting at prompt vengeance. Almost instantly Lescaut bursts in to warn that police are on their way. Even at this news, and though Des Grieux begs her to escape with him at once, Manon tarries to gather up her jewels. The delay proves disastrous; led by the gloating Geronte, the soldiers break in. The old man laughs sardonically at Manon when, in a panic, she drops her cloak, spilling the jewels on the floor. As Lescaut restrains Des Grieux, the girl is dragged off as a thief.

ACT III. On a street by the harbor of Le Havre, Des Grieux and Lescaut wait for the dawn, when they hope to rescue Manon from deportation to America as an undesirable. When she appears at the barred prison window, the lovers once again exchange vows but are interrupted by a lamplighter's plaintive song. At the sound of a shot, Lescaut, running in to say that the plot to abduct Manon has been uncovered, forces Des

Grieux to take cover. Soon soldiers lead in the women prisoners; as a sergeant calls the roll, they go on board ship, some defiant, some in tears. A curious crowd gathers and comments. Manon sobs farewell to Des Grieux, who begs the ship's captain in tears and desperation to let him accompany Manon; moved, the captain complies.

ACT IV. On a desolate plain in Louisiana, where they have fled after landing at New Orleans, the delirious and ailing Manon collapses, asking for water. When Des Grieux goes off in search of help and shelter, the girl is seized with terror and despair, haunted by her past. At his return, Manon dies in his arms, pledging that though her faults will be forgotten, her love for him will never die.

LA BOHÈME

ACT I. In their Latin Quarter garret, the near-destitute artist Marcello and poet Rodolfo try to keep warm on Christmas Eve by feeding the stove with pages from Rodolfo's drama. They are soon joined by their roommates—Colline, a young philosopher, and Schaunard, a musician, who brings food, fuel and funds. While they celebrate their unexpected fortune, the landlord, Benoit, comes to collect the rent. Plying the older man with wine, they urge him to tell of his flirtations, then throw him out in mock indignation at his infidelity to his wife. As his friends depart for the Café Momus, Rodolfo promises to join them later, remaining behind to try to write. There is another knock at the door; this time the visitor turns out to be a pretty neighbor, Mimi, whose candle has gone out in the drafty stairwell. Reviving her with wine when she feels faint,

Rodolfo relights her candle and helps her to the door. Suddenly Mimi realizes she lost her key when she felt faint, and as the two search for it, both candles are blown out. In the moonlight the poet takes the girl's shivering hand, telling her his dreams. She then recounts her life alone in a lofty garret, embroidering flowers and waiting for the spring. Rodolfo's friends are heard outside, urging him to join them; he calls back that he will be along shortly. Voicing their new-found rapture, Mimi and Rodolfo embrace and slowly leave, arm in arm, for the café.

ACT II. Amid the shouts of street hawkers, Rodolfo buys Mimi a bonnet near the Café Momus before introducing her to his friends; they all sit down and order supper. The toy vendor Parpignol passes by, besieged by eager children. Marcello's former girl friend, Musetta, enters ostentatiously on the arm of wealthy old Alcindoro. The ensuing tumult reaches its peak when, trying to regain the painter's attention, she sings a brazen waltz about her popularity. Complaining that her shoe pinches, Musetta sends Alcindoro off to fetch a new pair. The moment he is gone, she falls into Marcello's arms and tells the waiter to charge everyone's dinner to the old man. The bohemians fall in behind passing soldiers as Alcindoro returns to face the bill.

ACT III. At dawn on the snowy outskirts of Paris, a customs official admits farm women to the city. Late merrymakers are heard from within a tavern. Soon Mimi walks by, looking for the place where Marcello and Musetta now live. When the painter emerges, she pours out her distress over Rodolfo's jealousy and his intention of leaving her; it is best they part, she says. Rodolfo, who has been asleep in the tavern, is heard, and Mimi hides in the shadows, though Marcello thinks she has gone. The poet first tells Marcello that he wants to separate from his fickle sweetheart; pressed for the real reason, he breaks down, saying her cough can only grow worse in the poverty they share. Overcome, Mimi stumbles forward to bid her lover farewell as Marcello runs back into the tavern to investigate Musetta's promiscuous laughter. While Mimi and Rodolfo recall past happiness, Musetta races from the inn, quarreling with Marcello, who has caught her flirting. The painter and his mistress part in a fury, hurling jealous insults, but Mimi and Rodolfo decide to stay together till spring.

ACT IV. Separated from their sweethearts, Rodolfo and Marcello lament their loneliness in the garret. Colline and Schaunard bring a meager meal; to lighten their spirits the four stage a dance, which turns into a mock duel. The conviviality is abruptly ended by Musetta, who bursts in to say that Mimi is downstairs, too weak to climb up. As Rodolfo runs to her, Musetta tells how Mimi begged to be taken to her lover to die. While Mimi is made comfortable, Marcello goes with Musetta to sell her earrings for medicine, and Colline goes to pawn the cherished overcoat that has kept him warm so long. Alone, Mimi and Rodolfo wistfully remember their meeting and their first happy days together, but she is seized with coughing. When the others come back, Musetta gives Mimi a muff to warm her hands and prays for her life. Mimi dies quietly as Rodolfo lowers the blinds to soften the light. Schaunard suddenly notices that Mimi is dead and whispers to Marcello. Gradually Rodolfo realizes what has happened and runs to Mimi's side, calling out her name in despair.

TOSCA

ACT I. Cesare Angelotti, an escaped political prisoner, rushes anxiously into the church of Sant'Andrea della Valle, searches for and finds a key at the foot of a statue of the Madonna and hides in the Attavanti chapel. An old Sacristan shuffles in, praying in Latin at the sound of the Angelus. Then the painter Mario Cavaradossi enters to work on his portrait of Mary Magdalene, inspired by the Marchesa Attavanti (Angelotti's sister), whom he secretly sketches when she comes to pray at the family chapel. It was she who left the key at the statue and a disguise in the chapel for her brother. Mario contrasts the marchesa's blond beauty with that of the woman he loves, the raven-haired singer Floria Tosca. The Sacristan grumbles disapprovingly and leaves. Angelotti ventures out and is recognized by his friend and fellow liberal Mario, who gives him food and hurries him back into the chapel as Tosca is heard calling outside. She jealously questions Mario, then prays and reminds him of their rendezvous that evening at his villa, after her performance. Suddenly recognizing the Marchesa Attavanti in the painting, she explodes with renewed suspicions: "You see her, you love her, she loves you!" But Mario reassures her. When she has gone, Mario summons Angelotti from the chapel; a cannon signals that the police have discovered the escape, so the two flee to Mario's villa. Meanwhile, the Sacristan returns with choirboys who are to sing in a Te Deum that day. Their excitement is silenced by the entrance of Baron Scarpia, chief of the secret police, in search of Angelotti. When Tosca comes back to her lover, Scarpia shows her a fan he has just found, with the Attavanti crest on it. Thinking Mario faithless, Tosca tearfully vows vengeance and leaves as the church fills with worshipers. The amorous Scarpia has the diva trailed, scheming to get her in his power, while the church resounds with the Te Deum.

ACT II. In the Farnese Palace, Scarpia anticipates the sadistic pleasure of bending Tosca to his will. The spy Spoletta arrives, not having found Angelotti. To placate the baron he brings Mario, who is interrogated while Tosca is heard singing a cantata at a royal gala downstairs. She enters just as her lover is being taken to an adjoining room: his arrogant silence is to be broken under torture. Gradually unnerved by Scarpia's questioning and Mario's agonized screams, she reveals Angelotti's hiding place. Mario is carried in; Scarpia deliberately repeats Tosca's disclosure to Spoletta so that Mario turns on Tosca. The officer Sciarrone rushes in to announce that Napoleon has won the Battle of Marengo, a defeat for Scarpia's side. Mario shouts his defiance of tyranny and is dragged to prison. Scarpia, resuming his supper, suggests that Tosca yield herself to him in exchange for her lover's life. Fighting off his embraces, she protests her fate to God, having dedicated her life to love and art. Scarpia again insists, but Spoletta interrupts: faced with capture, Angelotti has killed himself. Tosca, forced to give in or lose her lover, agrees to Scarpia's proposition. The baron pretends to order a mock execution for the prisoner, after which he is to be freed; Spoletta leaves. Scarpia prepares a safe-conduct for the lovers. When he turns to embrace her triumphantly, Tosca stabs him with a dinner knife from the table, wrenches the document from his stiffening fingers and, as he dies, places candles at his head and a crucifix on his chest. Then she slips from the room.

ACT III. The voice of a shepherd boy is heard as church bells toll the dawn. Mario is led to the roof of the Castel Sant'Angelo prison to await execution; he bribes the jailer to convey a farewell note to Tosca. Writing it, undone by memories of love, he gives way to despair. But Tosca runs in, filled with the story of what she has done. Mario caresses the hands that committed murder for his sake and the two dare for a moment to hail the future. As the firing squad approaches, the diva coaches Mario on how to fake his death convincingly; the soldiers fire and depart. Tosca urges Mario to hurry, but when he fails to move she discovers that Scarpia's treachery has transcended the grave: the bullets were real. When Spoletta rushes in to arrest her for Scarpia's murder, Tosca climbs the battlements and, crying to Scarpia to meet her before God, leaps to her death.

MADAMA BUTTERFLY

ACT I. On a flowering terrace above Nagasaki harbor, U.S. Navy Lieutenant B. F. Pinkerton inspects the house he has leased from a marriage broker, Goro, who has procured him three servants and a geisha wife known as Madama Butterfly, or Cio-Cio-San. To the American consul, Sharpless, who arrives breathless from climbing the hill, Pinkerton describes the carefree philosophy of a sailor roaming the world in search of pleasure. For the moment, he is enchanted with the fragile Cio-Cio-San and intends to enter into a marriage contract for 999 years but subject to monthly renewal. When Sharpless warns that the girl may not take her vows so lightly, the lieutenant brushes aside scruples, toasting America and the "real" American wife he will one day marry. Cio-Cio-San is heard in the distance joyously singing of her wedding day. After she has entered, surrounded by her friends, she tells Pinkerton how, when her family fell on hard times, she had to earn her living as a geisha. Soon her relatives arrive and noisily express their opinions of the marriage. In a quiet moment Cio-Cio-San shows her bridegroom her few earthly treasures, telling him her intention of embracing his Christian faith. With pomp the Imperial Commissioner performs the wedding ceremony, after which the guests toast the couple. Suddenly Cio-Cio-San's uncle, a Buddhist priest, bursts upon the scene, cursing the girl for having renounced her ancestral religion. Pinkerton angrily orders priest and family to leave. Alone with his bride, he dries her tears and reminds her that night is falling. Helped by her maid, Suzuki, into a pure-white nuptial kimono, Cio-Cio-San joins the ardent Pinkerton in the moonlit garden, where love helps her to forget the lingering rejection of family and friends.

ACT II. Three years later, Cio-Cio-San waits for her husband's return. As Suzuki prays to her gods for aid, her mistress stands by the doorway, eyes fixed on the harbor. The maid shows Cio-Cio-San how little money is left but is told to have faith: one fine day Pinkerton's ship will appear on the horizon. Sharpless comes in with a letter from the lieutenant, but before he can read it to Cio-Cio-San, Goro, who has been lurking outside, brings in the wealthy Prince Yamadori, the latest suitor for her hand. The girl scornfully dismisses both, insisting that her American husband has not deserted her. When they are alone, Sharpless again starts to read her the letter and suggests as tactfully as he can that Pinkerton may not return. Wounded, Cio-Cio-San proudly carries forth their child, declaring that as soon as Pinkerton knows of his son he will surely come back. Moved by her devotion and lacking the heart to tell her of the lieutenant's remarriage, Sharpless leaves. Butterfly, on the brink of despair, hears a cannon boom; seizing a spyglass, she sights Pinkerton's ship, the *Abraham Lincoln*, entering the harbor. Delirious with joy, she tells Suzuki to help her strew the house with flower petals, which they gather in the garden. As night falls, Cio-Cio-San dons her wedding gown and she, Suzuki and the child begin their vigil, waiting for Pinkerton's return.

ACT III. As dawn breaks, Suzuki insists that Butterfly rest. Humming a lullaby to her child, she carries him to another room. Before long, Sharpless, Pinkerton and Kate, his new wife, enter. When Suzuki realizes who the American woman is, she collapses; out of care for her mistress, however, she agrees to aid in breaking the news to her. Pinkerton, overcome with remorse, bids an anguished farewell to the scene of his one-time happiness, then rushes away. No sooner is he gone than Cio-Cio-San comes forth, expecting to find him but finding Kate instead. She quickly guesses the truth. Leaning on Suzuki for support, she agrees to give up her child if his father will return for him. Then, sending even Suzuki away, she takes out the dagger with which her father committed suicide and bows before a statue of Buddha, choosing to die with honor rather than live in disgrace. Just as she raises the blade, Suzuki pushes the child into the room. Sobbing farewell, Cio-Cio-San blindfolds him and gives him a toy American flag to play with. Then, crouching behind a screen, she commits hara-kiri as the approaching Pinkerton is heard calling her name.

LA FANCIULLA DEL WEST

ACT I. At dusk in a California mining camp during the Gold Rush, the Polka Saloon fills with boisterous miners. The distant voice of Jake Wallace, an itinerant minstrel, is heard approaching; when he enters, the men join him in his nostalgic ballad. After money has been collected for young Jim Larkens, who longs to return home, Ashby, a Wells Fargo agent, arrives to tell the sheriff, Jack Rance, that he is about to close in on the bandit Ramerrez and his gang. As the bartender, Nick, serves drinks courtesy of Minnie, the Polka's barmaid and camp schoolteacher, Rance announces that she will soon be his wife. The miner Sonora jealously protests, and the ensuing brawl brings forth Minnie herself, who wrests Sonora's gun from his hand. After threatening to close the school if the men do not behave, she reads to them from the Bible. The mail arrives, and the miners go off to the dance hall to celebrate. Rance tells Minnie of his bitter life, empty of love and dominated by gold. In contrast, Minnie recalls the happy childhood she knew in her parents' saloon. Suddenly a handsome stranger enters, claiming to be Dick Johnson of Sacramento (but in reality Ramerrez). Remembering him from a brief romantic encounter on the road to Monterey, Minnie welcomes him. Suspicious, Rance and the miners challenge his presence, but Minnie vouches for Johnson and further infuriates the sheriff by dancing with him. Just then Ashby drags in Ramerrez' accomplice, José Castro, who, recognizing Johnson, leads a posse on a false chase to nab Ramerrez. When the men entrust their gold to Minnie, the love-struck Johnson, impressed with the girl's devotion to the miners, abandons his plan to rob the Polka. Instead, he accepts Minnie's invitation to her cabin and leaves.

ACT II. At the cabin, Minnie's maid Wowkle sings her papoose a lullaby as the father, Billy Jackrabbit, comes to discuss marriage. Soon Minnie enters; dismissing him, she excitedly gets dressed for Johnson's visit. When he arrives, full of compliments and advances, she begs him to slow down but, soon forgiving him, tells him of her happy life. After Wowkle leaves, he takes Minnie in his arms and kisses her. A mounting snowstorm leads her to suggest that he stay the night; Johnson retires to a bunk as Minnie curls up on a bearskin by the fireplace. As shots announce the posse's approach, Johnson hides. Rance, checking to see that Minnie is safe, tells her the stranger is Ramerrez, lover of the notorious Nina Micheltorena. Shocked, she sends the men away and turns on Johnson. Admitting his identity, he says he is a thief by birth, reared on stolen money, forced underground by his father's only legacy—a road gang. Since meeting her, however, he has changed. Touched, she nevertheless sends him away. Almost at once a shot rings out and Johnson staggers back, wounded. Scarcely has Minnie hidden him in the loft than Rance bursts in, hot on the trail. Not finding his prey, he makes advances toward

Minnie, who snatches his gun and orders him to leave. But drops of blood fall on his hand from the loft, revealing the bandit's hiding place. When Johnson climbs down, Minnie plays on Rance's gambling instinct by offering herself and her lover as stakes at poker. First hiding a full house in her stocking, she begins the game. Both win a round, but when Rance draws three kings in the winning third hand, Minnie pretends to faint; pulling forth the concealed cards, she defeats the sheriff, who leaves in a fury.

ACT III. By a dawn campfire in the forest, Rance regrets his bargain with Minnie. Harry and Handsome report the near capture of Johnson as savage outcries signal his continued pursuit; others shortly lead in the outlaw. From the vengeful miners, determined to hang him, Johnson begs one last favor: Minnie must not know his fate. Just as the noose is slipped around his neck, Minnie rides to the rescue. Holding her friends at bay, she reminds them of her years of devotion, in return claiming Johnson as her own. As a gesture of faith, she throws down her gun. All except Rance are won to her side. Johnson, freed from his bonds, thanks the miners, and he and Minnie leave California to begin a new life.

LA RONDINE

ACT I. At a soirée in Magda's elegant drawing room in Paris, Rambaldo and Magda are entertaining. The clever poet Prunier announces that sentimental love is fashionable again, a subtle germ that flies in the air. Accompanying himself at the piano, Prunier tries out his newest song, about a girl yearning for more than riches. Magda finishes the song; the girl falls in love with a student. Everyone is enchanted, and Rambaldo takes the opportunity to give Magda a pearl necklace. Prunier notices that Magda seems preoccupied and remote. Magda's friends envy her fortunate life with Rambaldo, but she counters with a memory of a beautiful man she met at Bullier's long ago. Pretending to read her palm, Prunier predicts that like a swallow, Magda may migrate to a life of love, only to return to the life she knows. The maid Lisette shows in Ruggero Lastouc, the son of one of Rambaldo's school friends. The guests decide that he must spend his first night in Paris carousing at Bullier's. The guests leave, including Rambaldo, who senses young Ruggero's attraction for Magda. Left alone, Magda finds Ruggero's list of nightclubs while recalling Prunier's prophecy. Her face lights up, and she rushes to her dressing room. It is Lisette's night off. Prunier meets her in the entrance hall and they leave, after flirting and embracing. Magda returns, dressed almost recognizably as a grisette. Putting a flower in her hair before the mirror, she slips out the door, bound for Bullier's.

ACT II. The ballroom at Bullier's is alive with flower girls, students, dressmakers, artists and drinkers. A group of flirtatious working girls crowd around Ruggero and try to guess his name, but he is irritated by them and brushes them off as Magda's arrival is noted by some students. Magda rids herself of these admirers by saying she has a rendezvous. Her eyes light on Ruggero, who returns her glance anxiously. When she joins him, he begs her to stay: so timid and alone, Magda reminds him of the girls back in Montauban. The two dance, enveloped by the crowd. Prunier and Lisette enter as Magda and Ruggero sit for a drink. Their long kiss is sighted by the chatterbox Lisette, but Magda catches Prunier's eye and gestures him to keep her quiet. He convinces Lisette she is mistaken: that is not Magda she sees but someone else. They join Ruggero at his table. When Magda admires Lisette's elegant clothes, the girl replies that she borrowed them all from her mistress. Soon, when Rambaldo comes in, Prunier tactfully removes Lisette and Ruggero. Rambaldo offers Magda his arm, but she refuses, saying that she has found love and intends to answer its call. Rambaldo bows to her: "May you not regret it." Dawn breaks as Ruggero comes back for Magda.

ACT III. The lovers are having tea on the terrace of their villa on the Riviera. It is a beautiful spring day. Magda is content with their existence, but Ruggero has written his father for permission to marry her, to legitimize their love. Ruggero tenderly paints a picture of their life together and runs off. Magda resolves to tell him her story, determined to be honest with him. When she has gone inside, the voices of Prunier and Lisette are heard. Prunier has tried unsuccessfully to put Lisette on the stage, but the girl would rather have her old job back. Magda greets them and takes Lisette back into her service. Prunier conveys to Magda a message from one who stands ready to help her: she should abandon the illusion she mistakes for happiness. The reference of course is to Rambaldo. Prunier departs, and Lisette goes into the villa. Ruggero runs in, elated that his parents agree to the match if his bride is pure. The tormented Magda undeceives him, telling him that she must leave him rather than bring him ruin. Like Prunier's "swallow," she must return to her former life. Leaning on Lisette, she finally leaves Ruggero, her one real love.

IL TRITTICO

IL TABARRO

Against a background of singing longshoremen and hooting tugboats, Giorgetta shares a few words with her husband, Michele, after another long day on their barge in the Seine. Michele tries to kiss his wife, but she turns away. Three stevedores, Talpa, Tinca and Luigi, join them for some wine. A passing organ grinder supplies music for an impromptu dance; then Michele returns to discuss business affairs with his wife. As a song peddler gives a sample of his latest tune to some girls, Talpa's ragpicker wife, Frugola, comes to collect him. After a day of rummaging she has a prize for Giorgetta—a good comb. For her cat, Caporale, she has a beef heart. Tinca leaves for the day, bound for the saloon to drink off his troubles. Luigi approves, for city life is hard and a man is better off not thinking about it. Mindful of the crowded city where poor people like Tinca are shoved in together, Frugola dreams of a little house in the country. But Giorgetta loves Paris; when Luigi agrees rapturously, it is apparent that the two are attracted to each other. When La Frugola and Talpa are gone, Michele comes back, rejecting Luigi's request to quit this job and find work in Rouen. Alone with Giorgetta, Luigi admits he wants to leave Paris because he cannot bear sharing her with her husband; they plan to meet later, and Luigi goes. Michele returns to sit on deck with his wife in the moonlight. Trying to bring Giorgetta close to him again, he recalls the joy they once knew with their child, now dead. She rejects his overtures and runs off. Gazing at the eternal Seine, Michele curses his ill luck. When he finds Luigi sneaking back on board, he forces a confession of love from his rival, then strangles him, hiding him in his cloak as Giorgetta returns to apologize for her behavior. But Michele opens his cloak to reveal the corpse of her lover, hurling her upon it.

SUOR ANGELICA

In the cloister of a Tuscan convent, a monitor deals out penances to late-comers and dismisses the sisters to their recreation. They sadly recall Bianca Rosa, who died the year before. Sister Dolcina (Sweet Tooth) confesses her longing for sweets, and Sister Genovieffa admits that she misses the little lambs she knew as a shepherdess. Sister Angelica turns away flustered, and a few of the women reveal she has not heard from her family for seven years. They say she was a princess, forced to enter the convent for an unknown crime. The sister nurse runs in, crying that Sister Chiara was stung by a bee; Angelica gives her herbs to cut the pain. Now two sisters enter with a donkey loaded with provisions—oil, nuts, cheese, eggs, butter and currants, the last of which thrill Dolcina almost to the point of venial sin. One of the nuns notices an imposing carriage outside, and the Mother Abbess tells Angelica that the visitor is her aunt. An aristocrat of the old school, the woman greets her niece coldly. She has brought a document for Angelica to sign, agreeing to the marriage of Angelica's younger sister. It was this aunt who sent Angelica to the convent for giving birth while yet unmarried. The tortured girl begs for news of her little boy and is told he died two years before. She collapses, sobbing, as the old woman prays; at length Angelica signs the document and is left alone to lament her child's death. Thinking only of how to join him in heaven, she uses her knowledge of herbal medicine to concoct a poison. Bidding the convent farewell, Angelica kisses the cross and takes her own life. Guilt-stricken because of her sin of suicide, she begs the Virgin for pity. In a vision, the dying Angelica sees Mary gently guide a little boy toward her.

GIANNI SCHICCHI

Grasping relatives of the wealthy Buoso Donati gather at his deathbed in thirteenth-century Florence to mourn his passing and investigate his bequests. Rumor has it that the old man has left nearly everything to a monastery, but if his will has not been filed there is still hope for the relatives, who begin a frantic search for the document. Young Rinuccio finds it and exacts a promise from his aunt Zita to let him marry his beloved Lauretta if there is enough money. She agrees, and the will is read:

everything is to go to the monks. Now the relatives are really in mourning, but Rinuccio suggests that Lauretta's father, Gianni Schicchi, a shrewd self-made man, can help them: his resourceful peasant stock will be the salvation of Florence, which the young man likens to a tree in flower. Schicchi appears with Lauretta. Disgusted by the hypocrisy and avarice he finds, he starts to leave but softens when Lauretta begs permission to marry Rinuccio. Reading the will, he first asserts that nothing can be done, then conceives of a plan to impersonate the dead man himself. Lauretta is sent from the room and the body removed from the bed. When the doctor pays a call, he is convinced by Schicchi's imitation of Buoso that the patient is better. Now Schicchi tells the others to send for the notary; donning Buoso's nightshirt and cap, he promises to dictate a new will. The relatives are overjoyed until they hear the tolling of a death knell. The bell, however, tolls not for Buoso but for one of the mayor's servants. Their greedy hopes renewed, the relatives get down to the business of bribing Schicchi to leave them the choicest items. He warns them they are all accomplices, the penalty for fraud being the loss of a hand and exile from Florence. When the notary arrives with witnesses, Schicchi bequeaths some of the property to the relatives but reserves the best for— Gianni Schicchi! The notary is hardly out the door when the enraged family falls on Schicchi and pillages the house while he chases them out. But the lovers, gazing rapturously out at the city, are happy. Schicchi's wits have provided them with a dowry and a house, and he turns to the audience to plead not guilty.

TURANDOT

ACT I. At sunset before the Imperial Palace in Peking, a Mandarin reads the crowd an edict: any prince seeking to marry Princess Turandot must first answer three riddles. Failure means death. The latest suitor, the Prince of Persia, is to be executed at the moon's rising; bloodthirsty citizens urge the executioner to sharpen his blade. In the tumult a slave girl, Liù, kneels by her blind old master, who has fallen from exhaustion. A handsome youth, Calaf, recognizes the old man as his long-lost father, Timur, vanquished king of Tartary. When Timur reveals that only Liù has remained faithful to him, Calaf asks why; she replies it is because once long ago he smiled at her. As the sky darkens, the mob again cries for blood but greets the moon with sudden, fearful silence and is moved to compassion when the Prince of Persia passes by and calls out to the princess, hidden in the palace, to spare him. Calaf too demands that she appear; as if in answer Turandot steps onto her balcony, with a contemptuous gesture bidding the execution proceed. The crowd falls prostrate, and she withdraws. As the death cry is heard from the distance, Calaf, transfixed by the beauty of this unattainable woman, strides to the gong that announces a new suitor. Three government ministers, Ping, Pang and Pong, rush to discourage him. When Timur and the tearful Liù also beg him to reconsider, Calaf tries to comfort them but breaks away to strike the fatal gong, thrice calling Turandot's name.

ACT II. In a palace pavilion, Ping, Pang and Pong lament Turandot's bloody reign, praying that love will conquer her icy heart and peace will return. The three let their minds float off to their beautiful country homes, but the noise of the populace gathering to hear Turandot question the new challenger calls them back to harsh reality. Before the palace the frail Emperor, enthroned high above, vainly tries to dissuade Calaf. Heralded by a chorus of children, Turandot appears to describe how her beautiful ancestor, Princess Lou-Ling, was brutally ravished and slain by a conquering prince; in revenge she has turned against men and determined that none shall possess her. Then, facing Calaf, she poses her first question: What is born each night and dies each dawn? "Hope," answers Calaf correctly. Unnerved, Turandot continues: What flickers red and warm like a flame, yet is not fire? "Blood," replies Calaf after a moment's pause. Shaken, Turandot delivers her third riddle: What is like ice but burns? A tense silence grips the assembly until Calaf triumphantly cries, "Turandot!" Defeated, the princess begs her father not to give her to the stranger, but to no avail. She asks Calaf if he still wants her against her will. Hoping to win her love, he responds with his own challenge: if she can learn his name by dawn, he will forfeit his life. Turandot accepts.

ACT III. In the palace garden Calaf hears a proclamation: On pain of death, no one in Peking shall sleep until Turandot learns the stranger's name. Ping, Pang and Pong try without success to bribe the prince to leave the city. As a mob threatens him with drawn daggers for the sacred information, soldiers drag in Liù and Timur; horrified, Calaf attempts to convince the crowd that neither knows his secret. When Turandot appears, commanding the dazed Timur to speak, Liù says that she alone knows the stranger's identity but will never reveal it. Tortured, she remains silent. Impressed by such endurance, Turandot asks what makes Liù strong; "love" is the girl's answer. When the princess signals the soldiers to intensify their torture, Liù snatches a dagger from one of them and kills herself. The crowd, fearing her ghost, forms her funeral procession. Turandot is veiled by her attendants and stands alone to confront Calaf, who at length rends the covering from her face and kisses her impetuously. In awe of his strength and warmth, Turandot weeps. The prince, now sure of his victory, reveals his identity. When dawn comes at last, the crowd assembles to hear of her victory or defeat. Turandot tells the Emperor that she knows the stranger's name: it is Love. The prince and Turandot embrace, hailed by the throng.

WORLD PREMIERES AND METROPOLITAN OPERA PREMIERES

LE VILLI

<table>
<tr><td>Teatro Dal Verme, Milan</td><td>Metropolitan Opera, New York</td></tr>
<tr><td>May 31, 1884</td><td>December 17, 1908</td></tr>
<tr><td>ANNA: Rosina Caponetti</td><td>ANNA: Frances Alda</td></tr>
<tr><td>ROBERTO: Antonio D'Andrade</td><td>ROBERTO: Alessandro Bonci</td></tr>
<tr><td>GUGLIELMO WULF: Erminoi Pelz</td><td>GUGLIELMO WULF: Pasquale Amato</td></tr>
<tr><td>CONDUCTED BY Arturo Panizza</td><td>CONDUCTED BY Arturo Toscanini</td></tr>
</table>

EDGAR

Teatro alla Scala, Milan
April 21, 1889
FIDELIA: Aurelia Cataneo
EDGAR: Gregorio Gabrielesco
TIGRANA: Romilda Pantaleoni
FRANK: Antonio Magini-Coletti
GUALTIERO: Pio Marini
CONDUCTED BY Franco Faccio

MANON LESCAUT

Teatro Regio, Turin	Metropolitan Opera, New York
February 1, 1893	*January 18, 1907*
MANON: Cesira Ferrani	MANON: Lina Cavalieri
DES GRIEUX: Giuseppe Cremonini	DES GRIEUX: Enrico Caruso
LESCAUT: Achille Moro	LESCAUT: Antonio Scotti
GERONTE: Alessandro Polonini	GERONTE: Archangelo Rossi
EDMONDO: Signor Ramini	EDMONDO: Jacques Bars
CONDUCTED BY Alessandro Pomé	CONDUCTED BY Arturo Vigna

LA BOHÈME

Teatro Regio, Turin	Metropolitan Opera, New York
February 1, 1896	*December 26, 1900*
MIMI: Cesira Ferrani	MIMI: Nellie Melba
RODOLFO: Evan Gorga	RODOLFO: Albert Saléza
MUSETTA: Camilla Pasini	MUSETTA: Anita Occhiolini
MARCELLO: Tieste Wilmant	MARCELLO: Giuseppe Campanari
SCHAUNARD: Antonio Pini-Corsi	SCHAUNARD: Charles Gilibert
COLLINE: Michele Mazzara	COLLINE: Marcel Journet
CONDUCTED BY Arturo Toscanini	CONDUCTED BY Luigi Mancinelli

TOSCA

Teatro Costanzi, Rome
January 14, 1900
TOSCA: Hariclea Darclée
CAVARADOSSI: Emilio De Marchi
SCARPIA: Eugenio Giraldoni
SACRISTAN: Ettore Borelli
CONDUCTED BY Leopoldo Mugnone

Metropolitan Opera, New York
February 4, 1901
TOSCA: Milka Ternina
CAVARADOSSI: Giuseppe Cremonini
SCARPIA: Antonio Scotti
SACRISTAN: Charles Gilibert
CONDUCTED BY Luigi Mancinelli

MADAMA BUTTERFLY

Teatro alla Scala, Milan
February 17, 1904
CIO-CIO-SAN: Rosina Storchio
PINKERTON: Giovanni Zenatello
SHARPLESS: Giuseppe De Luca
SUZUKI: Giuseppina Giaconia
GORO: Gaetano Pini-Corsi
CONDUCTED BY Cleofonte Campanini

Metropolitan Opera, New York
February 11, 1907
CIO-CIO-SAN: Geraldine Farrar
PINKERTON: Enrico Caruso
SHARPLESS: Antonio Scotti
SUZUKI: Louise Homer
GORO: Albert Reiss
CONDUCTED BY Arturo Vigna

LA FANCIULLA DEL WEST

Metropolitan Opera, New York
December 10, 1910
MINNIE: Emmy Destinn
RAMERREZ: Enrico Caruso
JACK RANCE: Pasquale Amato
JAKE WALLACE: Andrés de Segurola
CONDUCTED BY Arturo Toscanini

LA RONDINE

L'Opéra du Casino, Monte Carlo
March 27, 1917
MAGDA: Gilda Dalla Rizza
RUGGERO: Tito Schipa
LISETTE: Ines Maria Ferraris
PRUNIER: Francesco Dominici
CONDUCTED BY Gino Marinuzzi

Metropolitan Opera, New York
March 10, 1928
MAGDA: Lucrezia Bori
RUGGERO: Beniamino Gigli
LISETTE: Editha Fleischer
PRUNIER: Armand Tokatyan
CONDUCTED BY Vincenzo Bellezza

IL TRITTICO

Metropolitan Opera, New York
December 14, 1918

IL TABARRO
GIORGETTA: Claudia Muzio
LUIGI: Giulio Crimi
MICHELE: Luigi Montesanto
FRUGOLA: Alice Gentle

SUOR ANGELICA
ANGELICA: Geraldine Farrar
PRINCESS: Flora Perini

GIANNI SCHICCHI
GIANNI SCHICCHI: Giuseppe De Luca
LAURETTA: Florence Easton
RINUCCIO: Giulio Crimi
ZITA: Kathleen Howard

CONDUCTED BY Roberto Moranzoni

TURANDOT

Teatro alla Scala, Milan
April 25, 1926
TURANDOT: Rosa Raisa
CALAF: Miguel Fleta
LIÙ: Maria Zamboni
TIMUR: Carlo Walter
PING: Giacomo Rimini
PANG: Emilio Venturini
PONG: Giuseppe Nessi
CONDUCTED BY Arturo Toscanini

Metropolitan Opera, New York
November 16, 1926
TURANDOT: Maria Jeritza
CALAF: Giacomo Lauri-Volpi
LIÙ: Martha Attwood
TIMUR: Pavel Ludikar
PING: Giuseppe De Luca
PANG: Angelo Bada
PONG: Alfio Tedesco
CONDUCTED BY Tullio Serafin